AN INTRODUCTION TO

CELTIC
MYTHOLOGY

DAVID BELLINGHAM

For he comes, the human child,
To the waters and the wild
With a faery, hand in hand,
From a world more full of weeping
than he can understand.

(William Yeats, *The Stolen Child*)

For Sheree and the Riders of the Sidhe

A QUANTUM BOOK

Published by Grange Books
An imprint of Grange Books plc
The Grange
Grange Yard
London SE1 3AG

Copyright © 1990 Quintet Publishing Limited

This edition printed 1996

ISBN 1-85627-805-0

This book was produced by
Quantum Books Ltd
6 Blundell Street
London N7 9BH

Creative Director: Peter Bridgewater
Designer: Sally McKay
Project Editor: Judith Simons
Editor: Henrietta Wilkinson
Picture Researcher: Ruth Sonntag
Illustrator: Lorraine Harrison

Typeset in Great Britain by
Central Southern Typesetters, Eastbourne
Manufactured in Hong Kong by
Regent Publishing Services Limited
Printed in Singapore by
Star Standard Industries (Pte) Ltd.

itions: 'The bards celebrated the brave deeds of famous men in epic verse to the accompaniment of the sweet strains of the lyre.' Other sources as well as the later written versions of the myths themselves support Ammianus' statement, though 'epic' and 'lyre' were probably Graeco-Roman equivalents for whatever terms the Celts used. The original music and much of the epic poetry disappeared from the tradition when the myths were recorded by later Christian writers. However, some of the stories, dealing mainly with the heroic exploits of legendary Celtic warriors, have survived and make up the body of literature that we now call Celtic mythology.

Mythology can tell us many things about a society, ancient or modern. However, before we can begin to understand the nature of Celtic mythology, we must first of all deconstruct our own modern myth of the Celts. As can be seen from Yeats' early poems, during the late eighteenth and nineteenth centuries the main reference to Celtic myths was in Romantic texts: they provided a nostalgic escape from the Industrial Age back to an era ruled by 'nature' and 'magic' and peopled by heroic warriors and fair-skinned maidens. Each country's poets and painters rediscovered their own Celtic past: Ireland looked to pre-Christian legends such as the CuChulainn and Fianna (or Fenian) tales; Wales had the heroic saga of Pryderi in the *Mabinogion*; the Scottish poet James Macpherson (1736–96) forged his *Ossianic Ballads*, claiming them to be translations of a third-century Gaelic poet named Ossian; England resurrected the legends of King Arthur in works such as Tennyson's poem, *Idylls of the King*. The Romantic Age imbued the myths with their own romantic notions and often retained those elements of Christian medievalism which had become attached to the early written versions.

The Romantic vision of the 'Celtic Twilight' continues to influence our late twentieth-century perception of the Celts. We too require our dream-worlds and the word 'Celtic' conjures up mysterious moonlit landscapes with white-robed Druid priests performing strange rituals and brewing magic potions. Celtic art remains fashionable, particularly in jewellery: it has an abstract charm of its own and also signifies an attraction to an unknown past. Celtic literature weaves a similar spell: the narrator takes us from a world of seemingly real people and places into fantasy lands of fairies and monsters; his skill is such that we do not notice the transition. It is easy to be bewitched by such a culture.

We must ask whether the Celts themselves perceived their religion as a mystery and their poems as escapes from the real world. The answers are not readily forthcoming: the Celts did not write their own histories. Therefore, we have to learn about their customs and behaviour from the hands of contemporary Greek and Roman authors; although their view of the Celts was as mythical as ours, being based on the assumption that the Celts were uncivilized barbarians. Archeology has, however, confirmed some of the more extreme observations of the classical writers: the Celts do indeed appear to have performed human sacrifice and indulged in head-hunting. Archeology has also increased our knowledge of how the Celts lived, worshipped and buried their dead.

THE CELTS IN HISTORY

The earliest historical references to the Celts occur in Greek literature from around 500 BC. By this time they already appear to be inhabiting a wide geographical area, ranging from the upper reaches of the Danube in eastern Europe across to France and Spain. Archeological dating of Celtic finds

ABOVE **Gaulish stone with Celtic inscription** (*Vieux-Poitiers, France; c. first century* AD). *The ancient Celtic language has not survived as literature. Our knowledge of it comes from place-names, names of tribes and kings on coins and inscriptions carved on altars or sacred stones. The letter-forms were borrowed mainly from the Latin of contemporary Romans; Greek letters were sometimes used in southern Gaul.*

ABOVE **Irish cross-base inscribed with ogham and runic letters** (*Killaloe Church, County Clare, Ireland; c. 1000* AD). *The earliest Irish writings were in ogham script and date back to about the fourth century* AD. *Linear letters were carved on wood or stone across a central line and were differentiated by number and length of lines. Each letter was named after a tree or plant: for example 'd' was daur, meaning 'oak'. In Scandinavia, runic letters were used for the Teutonic (early Germanic) language. The oghams (right) read: 'A blessing upon Thorgrimr'; the runes (left) read: 'Thorgrimr carved this cross'.*

not only confirms the histories, but also informs us of the prehistoric Celtic past. A recognizably 'proto-Celtic' culture existed around the upper Danube in 1000 BC. However, some archeologists now argue for a widespread and gradual 'Celticization' of cultures which already existed in Bronze-Age northern and western Europe: thus, 'Celtic' Britain might date back to as early as 1500 BC, when the Wessex culture had the 'heroic' social features which conform with the early Irish Celtic myths.

Soon the eastern European 'Hallstatt' Celts were exploiting iron for tools and weapons and expanding their territories, firstly across Europe towards France and the Iberian Peninsula, as the early Greek historians affirm. The Gallic tribes then made incursions into Etruscan and Roman Italy, and having almost succeeded in besieging Rome in 387 BC, finally settled in the Po valley. The Celtic culture of this period is known as 'La Tène', after a site in Switzerland which demonstrates typical features of fifth-century BC Celtic society. Many archeologists see La Tène as the first truly Celtic culture, and certainly these are the people referred to from now on as Celts by the classical historians. Their military presence in northern Italy in the fifth

and fourth centuries BC is attested by Roman mythical accounts of the Gallic siege of Rome, which was apparently frustrated by the warning cackles of sacred geese; and some Etruscan funerary relief sculptures depict battles with Celtic warriors. A further Celtic expansion was directed towards southeastern Europe, the Baltic, and western Turkey. In the fourth century BC we find Alexander the Great receiving Celtic ambassadors at his Macedonian court; and in 279 BC we hear of Celtic tribes attempting to loot the Greek sanctuary at Delphi, defied by a miraculous fall of snow sent by the god Apollo.

The Greeks distinguished between the oriental Celts, whom they called *Galatoi* (Galatians originally from Gaul), and the Celts of western Europe whom they called *Keltoi*. The Romans made a further distinction by naming the French Celts *Galli* (Gauls), and the British Celts *Belgae* (originally from what is now Belgium) and *Britanni* (Britons). Celtic Gaul became the Roman province of *Gallia* after Julius Caesar's conquests in the first century BC and Britain became Roman *Britannia* under the emperor Claudius in AD 43. Ireland was never invaded by Rome and their myths therefore tend to preserve their earlier, prehistoric Celtic culture in more detail.

Julius Caesar and other writers of the first centuries BC and AD provide us with graphic accounts of Celtic culture and customs as seen by non-Celts. The main feature which emerges is that there was little unity among them: they were divided into aristocratic tribes ruled by chieftains who appear to have been constantly fighting one another. However, it must be remembered that the Romans probably encouraged such native tribal divisions to facilitate their own invasions.

ABOVE **Dedicatory inscription to Mars Mullo** (*Allones, France; late first century AD). After the Roman conquest of Gaul and Britain, native Celtic deities continued to be worshipped and were often combined with the imperial gods. This Latin inscription reads: 'To Augustus [Roman Emperor] and to Mars Mullo; Crescens the public servant has fulfilled his vow willingly and deservedly'. Mars Mullo was a Romano-Celtic mule god who was incorporated with the Roman war god, Mars. At Allonnes he was worshipped as a healer of eye disease: Mars was often seen as a peaceful healer in conquered territories.*

BELOW **The 'Dying Gaul'** (*Roman marble copy of Hellenistic bronze original of the second century BC). The Greek rulers of Pergamon (central Turkey) commemorated their victory over the Galatian Celts with a public monument depicting stereotypes of the defeated enemy. The Romans later copied the figures in marble, probably in celebration of their own victories in Gaul and Britain. The heroic chieftain is readily identified by his Celtic torc, moustache and bristling lime-washed hair.*

ANCIENT CELTIC SOCIETY

Caesar gives us a reasonably objective account of Celtic behaviour and dress in the first century BC. He tells us that the Celts lived in *oppida* or townships, some of which have been identified with the three thousand or so Iron-Age hill-forts of southern Britain; similar *oppida* existed in Europe and Galatia. Archeological evidence has allowed for reconstructions of the *oppida* dwellings, such as at Butser Hill in Hampshire, England. These were generally circular houses with wooden walls and thatched roofs; the banqueting halls of the myths would appear to be rectangular, though this may have been a medieval adaptation of the original story.

The Celts were primarily a warrior society ruled by warrior kings, queens and aristocrats, and the myths tell us nothing of the lower classes. They grew corn and herded cattle and learnt the use of coinage from the Greeks and Romans. Religious rituals played an important role in maintaining the social hierarchy of chieftains and tribes; the myths often presented and reinforced the sacred power of the Druidic priests, and the bards appear to have held equal respect. Both the myths and historical accounts reflect the Celtic pride of dressing up for battle: 'The Britons dye themselves with blue woad in order to appear more terrifying in battle. They wear their hair long, and their bodies are shaven except for the head and the upper lip.' (Caesar, *Gallic War V*). Herodian, writing in the third century AD, adds: 'As they are not used to clothes, they wear iron ornaments about their waists and necks, which they consider to be both decorative and a sign of wealth . . . they tattoo their bodies with abstract patterns and all sorts of animals.' Diodorus of Sicily,

ABOVE **Etruscans fighting Gauls** (*Etruscan alabaster funerary urn from Pieve, Italy; fourth century* BC). *The warriors are represented in an idealized classical Greek manner; the Greeks are distinguished from the Celts by their horses and helmets. The Etruscan language, like ancient Celtic, has only survived in brief inscriptions such as that above the scene.*

a contemporary of Caesar, describes the Celts as 'tall and muscular, with pale skin and blond hair which they highlight artificially by washing it in lime-water; they gather it back from the forehead to the top of the head and down to the nape of the neck . . . therefore the hair becomes so heavy and coarse that it looks like the mane of horses.' Classical representations of Celts conform with these literary stereotypes and archeologists have found tattoos on preserved Celtic flesh.

Caesar has little to say about Celtic women, except that they were 'shared between groups of ten or twelve men'. To the Romans and ourselves this would appear barbaric, but it may well imply a matriarchal system in which women had the social privilege of a number of lovers. Certainly high-ranking Celtic women enjoyed a degree of power unknown to their classical counterparts: witness the warrior queen Boudicca, who led the first-century AD rebellion against the Roman invaders. Although we must bear in mind that the Celtic myths were probably always told from a male viewpoint, the human female characters in Celtic mythology are rarely the downtrodden or faceless figures of the Greek myths, which might also suggest that, unlike in Classical Athens, free-born women formed part of the bard's audience.

THE CELTIC LANGUAGES

The pagan Celts spoke an Indo-European language which relates them in prehistory to the Greeks, Romans and Hindus. However, no record exists of the ancient languages, except brief inscriptions from the Roman period, and references in the classical authors to Celtic names. When the Celtic myths were finally written down in the early medieval period, the languages varied according to the author's country of origin: thus the Irish myths were recorded in Old Irish, but the contemporary Welsh form of the Celtic language would not have been understood by the Irish writers. It would appear that, by the time of the Roman invasion, any former cultural unity provided by a single Celtic language had disappeared: the Irish Celts were speaking 'Goidelic', while the British Celts were speaking 'Brythonic'. The Brythonic language seems to have been related to that spoken by the Gauls. Around the fifth century AD there were invasions and population movements in the western Celtic lands which led to linguistic changes: the Irish Goidelic language entered Scotland, later to become Scottish-Gaelic; the Anglo-Saxon 'English' language entered southern Britain, pushing the Brythonic language to Brittany.

THE SURVIVAL OF CELTIC MYTHOLOGY

Celtic myths were preserved in two main traditions: some were recorded by Christian writers and survive from the seventh century AD onwards while

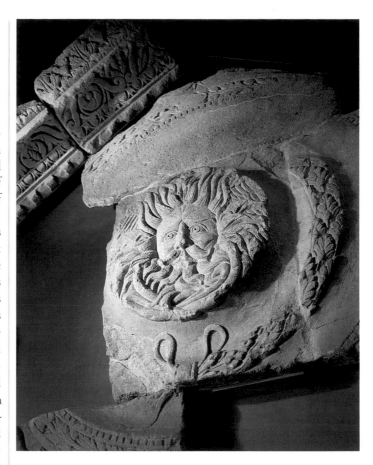

others have stayed alive in the oral folk traditions of Celtic areas. The apparent bias of the myths towards Britain and Ireland is due to the lack of surviving material from other former regions of the Celtic world, although surviving Celtic themes can often be observed in European folk-tales.

The earliest substantial survival of Irish mythology is a manuscript called the *Book of the Dun Cow*, containing versions from the CuChulainn sagas. Its Christian writer (author would be the incorrect term, implying an original creation) was a certain Maelmuri, whom historians know was murdered by Viking raiders in his cathedral at Clocmacnois in 1106. The curious title derives from a lost earlier manuscript of the seventh century AD written on cowhide (that of his pet cow!) by St Ciaran.

British mythology is now best known from the *Mabinogion* which was the title given by Lady Charlotte

ABOVE **Head of 'Medusa the Gorgon'** *(pediment of the Temple of Sulis Minerva, Bath, England; first century AD). The Greek female monster, with her snake-locks, was often used as an apotropaic figure in Greek and Roman religious contexts to 'avert the evil eye'. Here 'she' has become a 'he' complete with moustache and staring eyes in the Celtic style. Medusa's head was worn by Minerva on her breastplate to (literally!) petrify her enemies; her worship was combined with that of Sulis, the Celtic goddess of the healing waters of Bath. However, this 'Gorgon' has many unusual features, which may equally signify a Celtic sun deity, perhaps the consort of Sulis.*

Guest to her 1849 English translation of a collection of eleven Welsh tales preserved in earlier manuscripts: these are the *White Book of Rhydderch* of *c*1300–25 and the *Red Book of Hergest* of *c*1375–1425. *Mabinogi* means, broadly speaking, 'a tale of childhood': this was a mythical account of the conception, birth and early training of a Celtic hero. Lady Guest's word *Mabinogion* (which she incorrectly thought was the plural form) therefore implied that all eleven tales were of this genre. In fact only the first four 'Branches' are from an original *Mabinogi*; the other seven stories are of different genres and just happened to be included in the original manuscripts.

Celtic folk-tales survive in 'collected' versions recorded from the mouths of storytellers and singers by interested scholars. Unfortunately, with the advent of television in even the remotest areas of the Celtic world, the oral folk tradition is dying out. Although many of these folk-tales are simply good stories told by and for the rural community, there are some which preserve the 'high' myths and legends of the ancient Celtic ruling class.

THE NATURE OF CELTIC MYTHOLOGY

The bards were priests and teachers as well as entertainers and the behaviour of their mythical and legendary characters provided living Celts, both men and women, with ideals and thus ensured the continuity of the warrior society. Recurrent themes in Celtic mythology can therefore inform us about the preoccupations of their society. A love of beauty and bodily display is evident throughout the myths: when CuChulainn goes into battle, for example, his brightly coloured clothing, glowing jewellery and bristling hair are visual symbols of his heroic status. And heroines signify their own high and leisured status by wearing their hair in time-consuming intricate plaits, and by setting off their white unweathered skin with rich jewellery.

The world of nature was an unexplained and alien place to the Celts: therefore magical happenings tend to occur outside the stronghold, for example during the hunt; talking animals and birds feature in many of the stories; and Celtic divinities often represent the forces of nature. However, there is one important religious aspect which is often overlooked when we read the Celtic myths: scholars have demonstrated that the myths of other cultures tend to be narrative 'explanations' of historically attested religious rituals. Therefore, it is most likely that some of these stories were originally mythical explanations of religious mysteries or quests. So visits to the Otherworld might reflect an original rite of passage in which Celts passed from childhood to adulthood by means of a ritual period of absence outside the community. The Druidic philosophy encouraged a belief in immortality and the myths celebrate this idea: love persists beyond the grave in the form of intertwining trees on burial mounds; heads of dead heroes retain supernatural powers. Such beliefs were a consolation to the warrior society, where the hero's greatest glory was to die in battle.

Many elements in the surviving myths appear to mirror an earlier prehistoric 'heroic age' of Celtic culture, and thus the Celts of Caesar's day probably viewed their mythical ancestors with as much romantic nostalgia as did their admirers in the nineteenth century. However the myths also contain legendary representations of real historical characters, such as the fourth-century AD Roman emperor

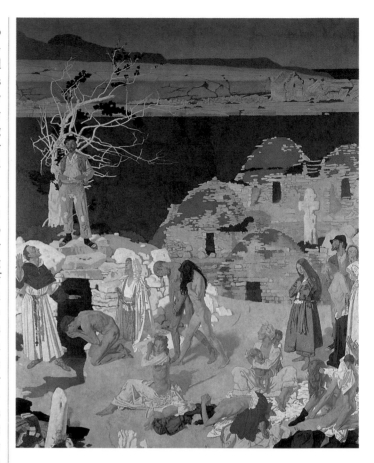

Magnus Maximus who appears as Macsen Wledig in the *Mabinogion*. This historical example suggests that mythical figures such as Pwyll and Branwen, though unknown in history, might also have once existed in prehistory as real persons whose deeds were outstanding enough to have been preserved in both bardic poetry and folk memory.

The mythical world remained so integral a part of Celtic society that when Christianity arrived, the spoken myths could not be destroyed. Instead they were often Christianized or given Christian endings: gods became God; the Druid priests of the old religion were overcome by the Saints of the new religion. The greatest wonder of these stories is that they have survived for so many centuries and provide an enchanting window into the rich and varied past of the Celtic West. These myths are now ours, and we should read, feel and learn from them before handing them on to our children.

ABOVE **The Holy Well** *(William Orpen; tempera on canvas, 1916). The Irish symbolist artist has depicted the 'beehive' huts of a Late Celtic Arran community. The islanders are being converted to Christianity in the waters of their pagan well; Orpen's artist friend Sean Keating stands above the well, apparently unconvinced by the new religion. The deserted crofter's hut in the background and the shamefully naked 'Adam and Eve' in the centre reinforce Orpen's criticisms of cultural change in Celtic places.*

CELTIC BRITAIN & IRELAND

PICTI

CALEDONIAN CONFEDERACY

Antonine Wall

DAMNONII
NOVANTAE
SELGOVAE
VOTADINI
Lindisfarne

ULSTER
Emain Machae

CARVETI
HADRIAN'S WALL

CONNAUGHT
Cruach
MEATH
kells.
ISLE OF MAN
BRIGANTES

Uisneach
Boyne
Tara.
Bruig Na Boinde (New Grange)
Clonmacnois
Liffey
SETANTII
PARISI

Shannon
LEINSTER
IRISH SEA
Anglesey
DIN LLIGWY
Alderley Edge
CORNOVI
CORITANI

MUNSTER
Harlech
DELI ANGLI
ORDOVICES
Severn
ICENI

BRITTANY

DEMETAE (DYFED)
Kitpeck
DOBUNNI
.Gloucester
CATUVELLAUNI
TRINOVANTES
Camulodunum

SILURES
Uffington White Horse
ATREBATES
Londinium
CANTIACI

Tintagel
Glastonbury.
BELGAE
Stonehenge
REGNENSES

DUMNONII
DUROTRIGES
Cadbury Castle
Butser

Maiden Castle

CELTIC EUROPE

THE EARLY CELTS

DIFFUSION IN 6TH AND 5TH CENTURIES B.C.

DIFFUSION IN 4TH CENTURY B.C.

DIFFUSION IN 3RD CENTURY B.C.

BRITAIN

TEUTONES
Rhine
Weser

Marne
Hallstatt

GAUL
LaTéne
Danube

NARBONESE GAUL

CELTIBERIANS
ETRUSCANS
.Rome
THRACIANS
GALATIA

Propontis
Delphi

13

ONE

The Saga of CuChulainn

The pagan Iron-Age Celtic world of Ulster (ancient Ulaid) is graphically preserved, albeit as a mythological fantasy, in the Ulster cycle of early Irish storytelling. The young hero of the tales was CuChulainn, who bears some resemblance to the Welsh Pryderi: both births are associated with colts which the heroes later own, and both are renamed later in life. These stories served as an education for young Celtic noblemen, the vivid heroic characters providing them with models of youthful warrior behaviour. Details such as the miniature weapons and sports equipment reflect the military and athletic training of them The following extracts from the saga of CuChulainn are taken from the twelfth-century manuscript known as The Book of the Dun Cow, *the earliest surviving written version of the tales of CuChulainn and the Ulster heroes. Various themes and mythical features of the stories suggest early pagan origins, with the Celtic gods Lugh and Cu Rui appearing in human guise. As in the tale of the Welsh Pwyll, the storyteller presents his audience with an apparently 'real' ancient Celtic world of hill-forts and recognizable place-names. However, the 'fairy' world is never far away: 'real' landmarks such as New Grange burial mound (ancient Bruig na Boinde) exert their magical influence, heroes are born, and superhuman deeds are performed.*

The story begins with the appearance of strange birds wearing silver chains. Like the chains worn by the Children of Lir, these are tokens of their fairy nature, and the storyteller uses them to transport the warriors, and the audience, into the Otherworld.

THE BIRTH OF CUCHULAINN

In the days when Conchobar was King of Ulster, his chieftains noticed a flock of birds feeding on the grass of the plain by Emuin Machae, and they fed until they had laid bare the land as far as the eye could see. The warriors were bird-hunters and they set out in their chariots to pursue the birds wherever they might lead them. Dechtire drove the chariot of her brother Conchobar, and nine chariots sped across the plain after the birds. A silver chain linked each pair of birds and their flight and song was so beautiful as to enchant the Ulstermen.

Evening drew near and the Ulstermen searched for shelter for it was snowing. They were welcomed into a cottage by a man who gave them food and drink, and the Ulstermen were merry by nightfall. Their host announced that his wife was about to give birth and asked Dechtire to help. The Ulstermen brought in from the snow a pair of new-born foals and presented them to the baby boy whom Dechtire was nursing.

In the morning the Ulstermen woke to the sight of the boy and his colts, but the strange birds and the house had vanished; they were just east of the Bruig. Back to Emuin Machae they went, where the boy grew for several years until he suddenly fell ill and died. Dechtire cried from her heart for the death of her foster-son. She asked for water and a copper bowl was brought to her, but every time she raised it to her lips a little creature would spring at her mouth from the water, and every time she looked into the bowl, nothing could be seen. Dechtire's sleep was broken by a dream of the man in the phantom house. He told her that his name was Lugh son of Ethniu and that he had lured her to the house and that she was now bearing the seed of his son: the boy was to be named

Setanta and given the two colts which were meant for him alone.

When the Ulstermen saw that Dechtire was with child they wondered whether the father might be Conchobar himself, for brother and sister slept side by side. Conchobar saved his embarrassment by betrothing his sister to Sualtam son of Roech. However, Dechtire was mortified at having to sleep with her husband whilst already bearing another man's child, so one night she lay alone and crushed the baby in her womb. But Dechtire soon became pregnant again by Sualtam and a son was born.

RIGHT **CuChulainn,** *(John Duncan, 1866–1945). The Dundee artist drew on the style and medievalism of the Pre-Raphaelites to create his images of the Celtic heroes of literature and folklore. His pencil drawing portrays the Irish hero with tartan cloak and late Celtic brooch. The image is seen from the front, which reflects Duncan's love of Byzantine art, while the dreamy eyes point to the influence of Rossetti and Burne-Jones. Duncan's inscription applies to both hero and artist: 'I care not though I last but a day if my name and my fame are a power forever'.*

THE BOYHOOD EXPLOITS OF CUCHULAINN (SETANTA)

Conchobar had lost the allegiance of several Ulster chieftains after he had slain the sons of Usnach. These men had gone across to Connaught on the west of Ireland. One of them, Fergus, recounted the childhood of Cuchulainn to his hosts Ailill and Medb, King and Queen of Connaught:

'He was brought up at Mag Muirthemni in the south of Ulster. One day Sualtam and Dechtire told their son of the famous boys of Emuin Machae, whom Conchobar watches at play when he is not playing the board games or drinking his way to bed. CuChulainn asked Dechtire if he could go and see the boys. "You must wait until an Ulster warrior can go with you," she replied.

'"I want to go now," said CuChulainn. "Which road must I take?"

'"Go northwards," answered his mother, "but take great care, for the route is filled with dangers."

'"I shall go anyway," said CuChulainn, and he set off with his toy weapons, a tiny spear and shield; he also took his hurley stick and ball, hoping to play a game with the boys of Emuin Machae.

'At Emuin he walked straight out onto the playing field without first asking for the protection of the other players. The boys were angry at this lack of courtesy, for we all know the rules of behaviour on the playing field. They told him to get off the field and threw their three fifties of spears at him (for they numbered one hundred and fifty): every spear stuck in the tiny shield of CuChulainn. They hurled three times fifty balls at him and each one he held to his

RIGHT **Din Lligwy settlement, Anglesey.** *The entrance (right) of this late Iron-Age (fourth century AD) circular hut faces the central courtyard of a small Celtic settlement. It consisted of two circular and seven rectangular dwellings surrounded by a limestone wall; two of these contained evidence of iron smelting in their hearths. The roofs would have been of thatch.*

chest. They threw their three times fifty hurley sticks at him, but he caught them all.

'CuChulainn was furious: the hairs on his head stood on end and sparkled with his rage. One eye he closed to the size of the eye of a needle, the other he opened to the size of a bowl. He grimaced so that you could see down his throat and his teeth gleamed from ear to ear. The moon of the great young warrior rose from his head. I myself was playing chess with Conchobar when in ran nine of the boys with CuChulainn in hot pursuit. Fifty of them already lay outside where he had struck them down. "This is not sporting," shouted Conchobar.

'"They are the bad sports," answered CuChulainn, "for I wanted to join in their games, and they tried to throw me off the playing field."

'"What is your name?" asked Conchobar.

'"I am Setanta, son of Sualtam and your sister Dechtire."

'"Why," asked Conchobar, "did you not ask for the protection of the other players?"

'"I have not been taught the rules," replied CuChulainn.

'"Then will you take protection from your uncle?" asked Conchobar.

'"I will," said CuChulainn, "but one thing I ask of you, that I be allowed to undertake the protection of the three times fifty boys." Conchobar agreed, and they all went out to the playing field and the boys whom CuChulainn had knocked to the ground arose at the sight of their new hero.'

Conall, another of the Ulster chieftains, continued the story:

'We knew the boy when we lived in Ulster, and it was a joy to watch him growing up. Soon after the episode at the playing field related by Fergus, CuChulainn was involved in more heroic adventures.

'Culann the blacksmith invited Conchobar to a feast. Not too many were to accompany the King of Ulster, for the smith had only the wealth

LEFT **Head of the Romano-British deity Antenociticus, from his shrine at Benwell, near Newcastle-Upon-Tyne, England** (*c. third century* AD). *This local Celtic god was worshipped in a small temple near a Roman military fort on Hadrian's Wall. The shrine provides evidence of the adoption of native divinities by Roman soldiers. The head is carved in the classical manner, but its Celtic features shine through in the powerfully modelled eyes and hair.*

produced by his hands and his tongs. Therefore only fifty favourite old champions were to accompany Conchobar. Before they left Emuin, the king paid a visit to the playing field to bid the boys farewell; CuChulainn was single-handedly playing the three times fifty boys, and he was winning. When they tried to fill the goal with their balls, CuChulainn defended on his own and stopped every ball. Afterwards, in the wrestling, he threw them all to the ground; yet all three times fifty of them could not pin him down. In the game of stripping, he had the clothes off the lot of them, without even losing his brooch.

'Conchobar wondered at the feats of his nephew and he asked his men whether CuChulainn would grow into a man and perform similar heroic deeds: they all agreed that this would be so. "Come with us to the feast of Culann," said Conchobar.

'"I shall finish the games", replied CuChulainn, "and follow after you."

'At the feast, Culann the smith asked his royal guest whether all were present. "Yes," answered Conchobar, forgetting his foster-son, "and we are ready to eat and drink."

'"Well then," said the smith, "let us close the doors and make merry; my dog shall guard the cattle in the

RIGHT **Wayland's Smithy, chambered long barrow, Oxfordshire, England** (c. 3500 BC). Wayland was the Norse smith god; legend stated that if a traveller left his horse at the site, together with a coin for payment, the horse would be shod and the money gone when he returned. Such ancient monumental tombs were often mythologized by the Celts who, like the later Danes, did not understand their original function.

fields: no man will escape him, for he requires three chains to hold him, and three men on each chain."

'Meanwhile, the boy was on his way to the feast, and to amuse himself he was throwing his ball in the air, and his hurley after it; and he was hurling his spear ahead and running to catch it before it hit the ground. As he entered the courtyard of Culann the smith, the dog went for him. The disturbance was heard by Conchobar and his men, and they watched from the windows as CuChulainn fought the dog with his bare hands. He held it by the throat and back and smashed it to pieces against a pillar. CuChulainn was taken into the house. "I am glad for your mother's sake," said Culann, "that you are alive. But that dog protected all my goods, and now I am done for."

'"Fear not," said CuChulainn; "I shall raise a puppy of similar pedigree for you, and until it is large enough to guard your property I myself shall be your watchdog."

'"Then we shall call you CuChulainn, 'The Hound of Culann', from now on," said Conall.

'Such were the exploits of a boy of six,' said Conall. 'What mighty deeds can we expect of him now that he is seventeen?'

THE FEAST OF BRICRIU

Bricriu 'Nemthenga' ('Poison-Tongue') invited Conchobar and the Ulstermen to a magnificent feast in a beautiful house designed specially for the occasion. Opposite the house Bricriu built a cottage with large glass windows so that he could see into the house, for he knew that the Ulstermen would not allow him to dine with them.

Before the feast Bricriu visited Loegaire, Conall Cernach and CuChulainn, three of the greatest heroes of Ulster, and told them of a prize which would be reserved at his feast for the champion of champions: 'You will become king of all Ireland,' Bricriu told each hero, 'if you win the champion's prize. You will receive a cauldron large enough to hold three warriors full of wine. You shall have a boar fed for seven years on milk and grain in the spring, curds and sweet milk in the summer, wheat and acorns in the autumn, and meat and soup in the winter. And you shall have a noble cow which for seven years has grazed on heather and milk, meadow-herbs and corn. And you shall have in addition one hundred large honey-cakes. This is the prize intended for you alone, for you alone are the greatest of the Ulstermen. You are to claim the prize as the feast begins.' So Bricriu tempted each hero and returned to finish the preparations for the feast.

The Ulstermen arrived on the day appointed for the feast, and each man and woman took their place in the great hall according to their rank. When all was ready the musicians began to play and Bricriu announced, 'Over there is the portion reserved for the champion. May the best man win.' And with those words he left the hall and entered his cottage.

LEFT **Chariot-burial of young adult female, Wetwang, Yorkshire, England** (c. second to first centuries BC). A square barrow marked the grave. The wheels and shaft can be seen alongside bronze female goods, including a mirror and work-box; a side of pork, often mentioned in mythology as 'the champion's joint', was included for the underworld meal. A similar male burial was found nearby, his Celtic warrior status signified by sword, spears and shield.

BELOW LEFT **Handle of bronze bowl, Hallstatt, Austria** (sixth century BC). An early example of Celtic metalwork. The myths abound with descriptions of such fine metal vessels at aristocratic banquets. The cow and calf are solid cast bronze and are depicted in a geometric style typical of Hallstatt art.

As Bricriu had hoped an argument began immediately between Loegaire, Conall Cernach and CuChulainn, and soon the three warriors were fighting. Conchobar stepped between them and Senchae, who was the oldest and wisest of the Ulstermen, said, 'We should not have fighting during the feast. Tonight the portion shall be divided between all three of you, and tomorrow we shall ask Ailill, King of Connaught, to settle the dispute.' All agreed with these words of wisdom and soon the company was merry with food and wine.

Meanwhile Bricriu was scheming in his cottage as to how he might set the great women of Ulster against one another. At that moment Fedelm, wife of Loegaire, came out of the house. 'Surely,' said Bricriu, 'you are wife of the greatest hero of Ireland. If you lead the women of Ulster back into the house tonight, you will forever be first lady of Ulster.' And Bricriu made the same promise to Lendabair, wife of Conall Cernach, and to Emer, wife of CuChulainn. The time came for the women to rejoin their husbands in the hall. They started walking at a stately pace, but as the house came in sight, they walked faster and faster until soon they were hitching up their dresses and running. The Ulstermen heard the commotion and, thinking that they were being attacked, barred the doors of the hall. The women hammered on them from the outside, as each wanted to become the first lady of Ulster. CuChulainn used his great strength to lift up a wall of the house and Emer was thus able to slip into the feast and claim her prize.

The feasting continued but soon the three heroes and their wives began squabbling once more over the

19

RIGHT **Gold amulets from Szarazd-Regoly, Hungary** (c. 100 BC). *These fine examples of miniature Celtic metalwork are formed from embossed gold-leaf with filigree and granulated decoration. The wheel symbolized the sun god and was used in burials as a protective talisman against the forces of darkness.*

champion's prize. It was decided that the three should journey in their chariots to either the King of Munster, Cu Roi, son of Daire, or to Ailill and Medb, King and Queen of Connaught: one of these would settle the dispute. They raced one another westwards across the hills and plains towards Connaught and Munster, and the ground shook beneath them.

Medb heard the commotion from the citadel at Cruachu and asked her daughter Findabair to go to the gatehouse tower of the fort and describe who was coming in such great fury: 'In the first chariot I see a man with long hair: he wears it in braids and from root to tip it changes colour from brown to blood red and golden yellow.'

'That is surely Loegaire,' said Medb, 'and he will slay all in Cruachu.'

'In the next chariot stands a man with the loveliest hair: like the manes of his horses is it braided, and his face glistens with red and white hues. He wears a blue and crimson cloak, and carries a shield with bronze edge and yellow boss; in the other hand he holds a spear of burning red, and the birds swoop around him.'

'That must be Conall Cernach,' said Medb, 'and he will cut us all to pieces.'

'And the third chariot,' continued Findabair, 'is pulled by the swiftest of horses: one is grey and one is black, and they run faster than the birds and they breathe flashes of lightning. And the warrior is a sad, dark man, the most beautiful man in Ireland; I see his white breast beneath his scarlet tunic, fastened with a golden brooch; his eyes gleam with jewels of dragon-red, and his brilliant red cheeks are aflame as he leaps like a salmon above his chariot.'

'That is CuChulainn,' cried Medb, 'and we shall be ground to dust by his rage.'

Medb welcomed the heroes with a vat of water to cool them off and fifty women to attend them in their guestrooms. They then told Ailill and Medb that they had come to seek their judgement in the dispute over the prize of Bricriu; and all cursed Bricriu for his troublemaking.

Ailill could not make his mind up about the three contestants, so Medb took the judgement upon herself: 'There is no difficulty at all in judging them,' Medb told her husband, 'for Loegaire is as different from Conall Cernach as tawny bronze is from white gold, and Conall Cernach is as different from CuChulainn as white gold is from red gold.' She summoned Loegaire: 'I consider you to be king of all Ireland,' said Medb, 'and you are to have the champion's prize; you are to return to Conchobar and the Ulstermen and show them this as a token of our choice.' And she gave him a bronze cup, its base decorated with a bird in white gold, and Loegaire drained the wine in it, and joined his fifty women in bed.

Medb then summoned Conall Cernach, and said the same to him, and gave him a white gold cup with a golden bird on its base. He too drained the wine and went to bed; his fifty women were joined by Sadb Sulbair, daughter of Ailill and Medb.

Finally she summoned CuChulainn, and Ailill joined her in judgement. To the hero was given a cup of red gold, and the bird on its base was carved from a priceless gem. 'You are champion of champions,' said the King and Queen of Connaught, 'and your wife Emer is in our opinion the first lady of Ulster. Return to Conchobar tomorrow and claim the prize.' CuChulainn was joined in bed by Princess Findabair.

Before their departure on the next morning, the heroes entertained the court with their competitions. They played the game of throwing the wheel: Loegaire only managed to reach the top of the wall of the hall; Conall Cernach hit the ridge-beam to the cheers of the youth of Connaught; but CuChulainn's throw hit the ridge-beam so hard that the wheel flew out of the roof and landed an arm's length into the ground outside. CuChulainn then took the needles from the three times fifty women, and threw them one by one into the air, so that each was threaded in the eye of the next to form a chain. He returned each needle to its owner to the cheers of the crowd that had gathered in the courtyard. The three heroes then bade farewell to Ailill and Medb and the people of the fort of Cruachu and each returned separately to Ulster.

Conall Cernach and CuChulainn were held up by various adventures and when they eventually reached

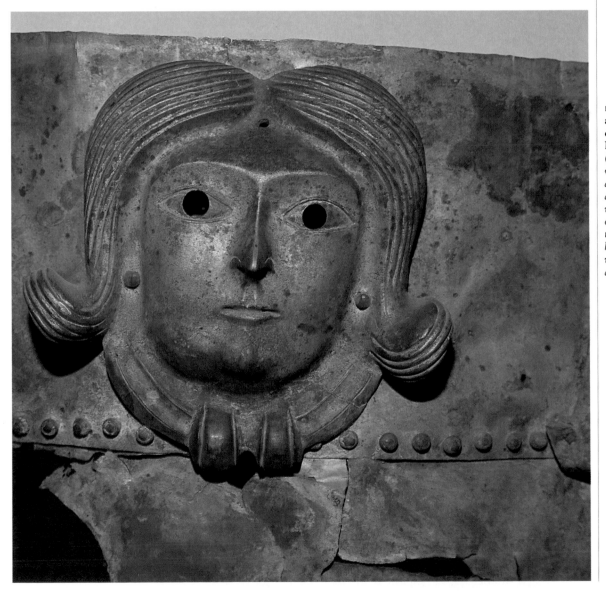

LEFT **Human head on a large bronze cauldron from Rynkeby, Denmark** (*first century* BC). *He wears the warrior torc, and his stylized features are typical of Celtic representation. Heads of oxen also decorate this cauldron, and may have signified its use as a ritual container for animal sacrifice.*

Conchobar's fort at Emuin Machae, they found the court in mourning: Loegair had arrived before them and falsely announced their deaths. The bickering which ensued was halted by Sualtam, father of CuChulainn, who called everyone in for a homecoming feast. 'Why not let another hero claim the champion's prize?' said one of the Ulstermen during the merry-making. 'After all, if any of these three had been chosen during their stay at Cruachu, he would have brought home a token as proof.' At this challenge Loegaire produced his cup and claimed Bricriu's prize. 'The prize is for me,' said Conall Cernach, taking out his cup, 'for mine is a golden cup and yours is only bronze.'

'Then I am champion of champions,' cried CuChulainn, and he showed the company the red–gold cup with its precious-stone bird.

'Ailill and Medb have judged,' shouted Conchobar and the Ulstermen. 'We award you the champion's prize.' But Loegaire and Conall Cernach refused to acknowledge the decision and accused CuChulainn of bribing Ailill and Medb. Out came the swords once more. Conchobar stopped the fight and Senchae the Wise pronounced that the three should go to Cu Roi of Munster for his final judgement.

When they reached the fort of Cu Roi, they found that he was away from home, but Blathnat his wife had been instructed to wine and dine them until her husband's return. After dinner Blathnat told the three that each night one of them must take the night-watch, according to Cu Roi's bidding. That night was the turn of Loegaire, for he was the eldest. The moment the sun had set, they felt the fort revolve like a water-wheel for Cu Roi put a spell on it every night, so that no enemy might find its entrance gate after dark.

Loegaire stood watch while the others slept. As it began to get light, a giant emerged from the ocean in the west. Though he was far away, the giant seemed to Loegaire as tall as the sky. As he advanced, Loegaire noticed huge tree trunks in his fists, which he hurled at Loegaire. They missed their target and the raging giant picked Loegaire up like a baby in his fist and crushed him as if between two mill-stones. The giant dropped Loegaire over the walls of Cu Roi. When the others found his half-dead body, they thought he had tried to leap the walls as a challenge to the other men.

On the following night it was the turn of Conall Cernach to watch and the same giant caused the same injuries that had befallen Loegaire. The next night was for CuChulainn and it was an evil night, for it had been prophesied that a monster from the lake beneath the citadel would devour all who dwelt there. Just before sunrise there was a great thrashing of water which startled CuChulainn who was half asleep. He looked over the walls and saw the monster, who rose high above the lake. It turned its head and attacked the fort, opening its huge mouth to swallow hut after hut. CuChulainn leapt high into the air, thrusting his arm down the beast's throat and tearing out its heart.

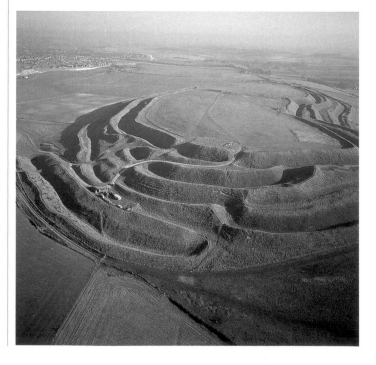

BELOW **Maiden Castle hillfort, Dorset, England** (c. 300 BC). *The stronghold of the Durotriges Celtic tribe has a long and complex building history, dating from around 2500 BC, but only reaching its present size in the Celtic period. The remarkable winding approach to the main entrance proved of little defence when the Romans stormed the fort in the first century AD. The site continued thereafter as a religious centre: a circular timber temple was rebuilt in stone together with a square stone temple in the fourth century AD.*

The hero hardly had time to rest before he too saw the giant rising from the ocean. The giant threw his tree trunks and CuChulainn threw his spear: all missed their targets. The giant then tried to grasp CuChulainn in his fist, but CuChulainn was too quick, and he performed his salmon leap and circled the giant with his sword. 'I'll give you anything, if you spare my life,' said the giant. 'I want the champion's prize and Emer to be first lady of Ulster,' said CuChulainn. 'Granted!' called the giant as he disappeared into the morning mists.

ABOVE **Celtic god on outer panel of the Gundestrup Cauldron, Denmark** (first century BC). This gilt-silver cauldron was found in a bog in Denmark, outside the boundaries of the Celtic world; but its mythological images are undoubtedly Celtic. Here, a colossal god demonstrates his power over men holding wild boars. The boar and pig were sacred animals, often used for important sacrifices; and were also employed as warrior symbols in the form of helmet crests.

Cu Roi returned the next day and heard about the great deeds of CuChulainn. He accordingly granted him the prize of champions and the three heroes of Ulster set off for home. And once more Loegaire and Conall Cernach refused CuChulainn the prize, but CuChulainn was weary of the contest and the matter was allowed to rest.

Some time later, Conchobar and the Ulstermen were about to dine at Emuin Machae when a hideous ogre appeared at the door and challenged them to the game of beheading. The three great heroes were absent and Muinremur accepted the challenge. 'The rules are these,' cried the giant, 'you cut my head off tonight and I cut off yours tomorrow.'

'Fair enough!' laughed Muin-remur, who had no intention of keeping his side of the bargain with the foolish ogre. The ogre laid his head on the chopping block and Muin-remur sliced off his head with an axe. To the surprise of them all, the ogre arose, took his head and walked off, saying that he would be back the next day. The following evening he returned but Muinremur was nowhere to be seen. The ogre protested at the outrage and another warrior agreed to make the same bargain. On the following night that warrior also kept out of the way of the ogre. This happened for three nights and on the fourth night many people gathered in the court to witness the marvel. CuChulainn was present and the ogre challenged him to the game of beheading. CuChulainn not only knocked his head off with one blow but he also smashed it to bits on the floor. Even so the ogre arose, picked up the pieces and left. The following evening the ogre returned, knowing that CuChulainn was a hero who kept his word. 'Where is the hero CuChu-lainn?' asked the ogre.

'I shall not hide from the likes of you,' answered CuChulainn.

'You sound worried,' said the ogre, 'but at least you have kept your word.' CuChulainn laid his neck on the block and the ogre raised his axe; everybody gasped and turned away. As he brought the axe down, the ogre turned the blade so that only the haft caught CuChulainn on the neck.

'Now rise up, CuChulainn!' cried the ogre, 'for of all the heroes in Ulster and indeed in the whole of Ireland, you are the greatest in terms of valour and honour. You are champion of champions and the prize of Bricriu is for you alone. Your wife Emer is the first lady of Ulster. And if any of you dispute this fact, your days will be numbered.' With these words the ogre left the room, but as he left he was transformed into Cu Roi, son of Daire, and thus ensured that his judgement of the three heroes was to be final.

BELOW **The Death of CuChulainn** (bronze sculpture by Oliver Sheppard, The General Post Office, Dublin, Ireland; erected after the 1916 Easter Uprising). The Irish hero was eventually mortally wounded by a spear thrown by his enemy Lugaid. In his desire to die upright and fighting he lashed himself to a stone pillar. Lugaid only dared to approach when the crow settled on his shoulder, signifying death. The head of the hero was buried beneath a mound at Tara. This public memorial symbolizes those who have died in the fight for Irish independence.

Celtic Art

The eye-catching quality of Celtic art reflects a society which placed great importance on visual displays of its wealth. The style is at its most characteristic in the abstract curvilinear patterns used as ornamentation on a wide range of objects. The early Celtic craftsmen established a basic repertoire of attractive decorative patterns. These patterns, though to our modern eyes 'abstract' and therefore without obvious meaning, must have provided the ancient Celts with a powerful visual sign of cultural identity: the same patterns are found throughout the Celtic world.

The remarkable resilience of this decorative style to external changes in Celtic culture can be gauged by its survival through time. The unmistakable taut, curving

ABOVE **Cernunnos and beasts** (*inner plate on the Gundestrup Cauldron, Denmark; first century* BC). *A rare example of figurative art from the La Tène period. The silver cauldron had thin gold foil applied over its exterior scenes. The silverworking techniques were learnt from the eastern Celts; the images were carved into metal or bone dies, and the bronze plate was then hammered into the dies from behind (repoussé); further details were then chased onto the surface with punches and engraving tools. The scenes and mythical characters are Celtic: Cernunnos the antlered god appears with stag, boar, bull, ram-horned snake and La Tène style torc.*

lines of Celtic art can be traced in an unbroken tradition from the eighth century BC with the early 'Hallstatt' culture in eastern Europe. The style appeared in Britain in the third century BC, with the 'La Tène' culture and survived some fourteen hundred years through to the Norman conquests. Various chronological changes in the basic style as well as regional variations have been identified by art historians. The style never completely disappeared from artistic production in those areas which retained a strong sense of their Celtic past. Ireland and Scotland have been particularly successful in reviving the art at different times of their post-Norman history, and nineteenth-and twentieth-century metalworkers have continued to find a market for Celtic jewellery designs.

The Celtic craftsmen seem to have left storytelling to the poets, and there is little that can be called 'narrative' in Celtic art. In place of the representation of heroic adventures found for example in ancient Greek art, the Celtic artists attracted the eye with what were often highly intricate interwoven linear forms: these forms range from simple threaded lines through to complex fantasies drawn from the natural world. When human or animal forms do appear, the naturalistic representations of Classical western art are avoided, and nature is interpreted in a strikingly stylized, even distorted manner.

The fantastical and sometimes bizarre forms of this art should be seen in the overall context of Celtic culture. The sheer time and skill involved in creating such complex forms in stone, wood and metal provided the tribal leaders with visible signs of their dominant position in Celtic society. The wealthy men and women who wore and handled these art objects also commissioned the storytellers, and the myths themselves rely on a similar interweaving of plots and sub-plots to hold the listeners' attention; likewise, mythical narratives are peppered with marvellous incidents and occasional shocks. The mysteries of Druidic religious ritual were at the core of Celtic thought, and this also must have affected the artistic tendency to avoid direct images of gods and men.

OPPOSITE **The Trundholm Chariot** *(from a fen in Denmark; c. 1300 BC). The religious themes, artistic styles and materials of Iron-Age Celtic art have their roots in the Bronze Age. This bronze model of a horse and gold-plated disc probably symbolized the sun: horse and sun symbols appear together on later Celtic coins.*

ABOVE **Head from Msecke Zehrovice, Czechoslovakia** *(limestone; c. third to second centuries BC). This eastern Celtic head was discovered beside a religious shrine and was probably an offering to a god, but whether it represents deity or worshipper is uncertain: the torc, symbol of a warrior chieftain, would suggest the latter. The staring eyes and stylized curvilinear features are typical of La Tène art.*

ABOVE LEFT **Electrum torc** (from Snettisham, Norfolk, England; first century BC). Eight twisted wires make up each of the eight main strands; these were soldered onto the terminals, which were decorated with curving La Tène style ornaments. The British artists developed an increasingly insular version of the continental style.

BELOW LEFT **Irish silver penannular brooch** (seventh century AD). This type of brooch was exported from pre-Roman Celtic Britain to Ireland. By the early medieval period the Irish Celts were making their own extremely rich examples.

LEFT **Base of the Cross of Cong** (County Mayo, Ireland; bronze and oak; twelfth century). The Viking invaders influenced Late Celtic Irish art with its interweaving tendrils and dragons. The use of a beast to support the cross symbolizes the triumph of Christianity over 'nature'. The cross was made for the High King of Ireland, Turlough O Conna.

RIGHT **Horse mask** (from Stanwick, Yorkshire, England; first century AD). This bronze fitting was one of a number of horse trappings from the Celtic tribal centre of the Brigantes, destroyed by the invading Romans. The unnaturalistic features are typical of this period.

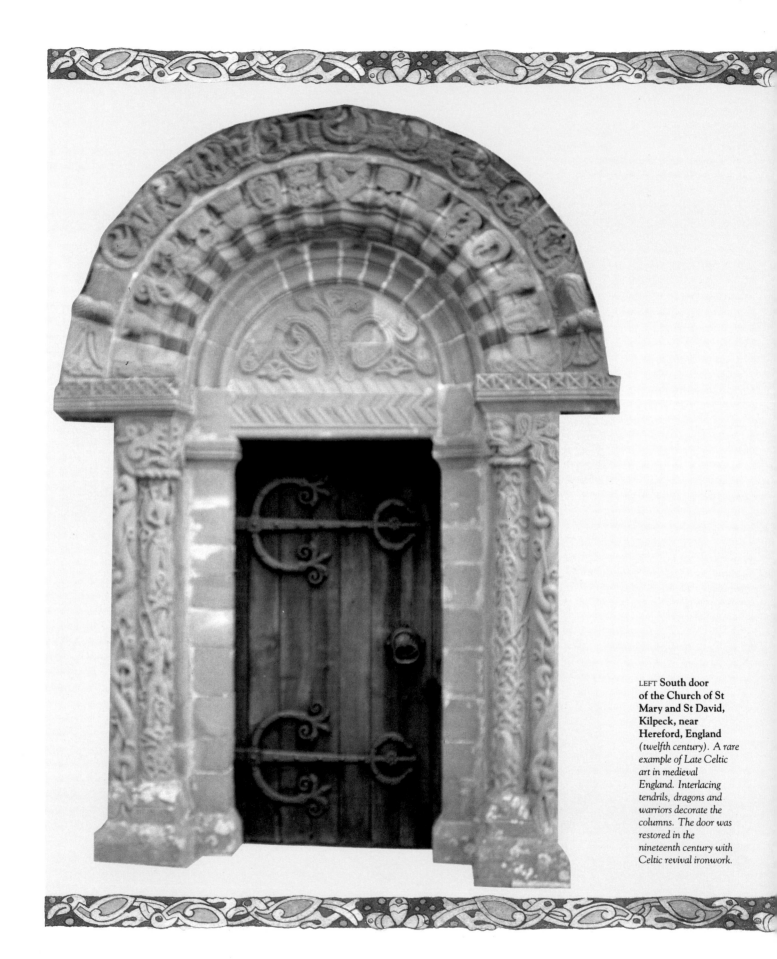

LEFT **South door of the Church of St Mary and St David, Kilpeck, near Hereford, England** *(twelfth century). A rare example of Late Celtic art in medieval England. Interlacing tendrils, dragons and warriors decorate the columns. The door was restored in the nineteenth century with Celtic revival ironwork.*

The pagan Celts took their most treasured possessions into the grave and the finest examples of Celtic art appear in aristocratic tombs. Clothing accessories for both men and women, such as brooches, neck collars, torques and armlets, were of rich metals. Gold, silver or bronze were cast in flat moulds bearing Celtic designs or the metal was simply twisted and sometimes plaited to create more complex forms; some torques consisted of hollow tubes. Colour was provided by enamel inlays. Bronze hand-mirrors have been found mainly in women's graves, their backs incised with Celtic designs. Finely decorated metal horse-tackle, drinking bowls, swords, shields and helmets reflect the fighting and feasting of the myths and female as well as male chariot-burials provide evidence of the strong position of women in the Celtic warrior society. Celtic art also manifested itself in stone carvings connected with tombs and religious sites, but the most monumental expressions of the style are the huge figures carved into the chalk of downland hills: these have been interpreted as religious images or tribal emblems.

The work of Celtic craftsmen under Roman rule kept the artistic tradition alive: Celtic and Roman artistic styles can often be identified in the same art object. The Romans never penetrated Ireland and it is perhaps ironic that the 'golden age' of Celtic art occurred not under the patronage of pagan chieftains but within a Christian context. New metalworking techniques of filigree and granulation were learnt by the Irish artists in the seventh century AD. The old pagan interlaced designs now appeared on objects of Christian ritual – crosses, chalices and patens for Communion; reliquaries for the bones of saints; bishops' crooks as signs of the new spiritual leaders; and decorative letter-headings in Christian manuscripts. The richest Celtic brooches are also from this late period.

The most recent revivals of Celtic visual art occurred mainly in the works of late nineteenth-century Scottish painters such as John Duncan. They incorporated the old Celtic patterns into the clothing and furniture of scenes from the Celtic myths. These artists tended to romanticize the myths, according to the taste of their day. In the more recent Celtic revival, the artwork of the Devon painter Alan Lee has provided new romantic evocations of the ancient Celtic world in his book-illustrations of Welsh and Arthurian myths. Lee, like Duncan, has drawn on the decorative patterns of earlier Celtic artists to imbue his more realistic images with an authentic Celtic flavour.

LEFT **The Riders of the Sidhe** (*John Duncan; tempera on canvas, 1911). The Sidhe (Shee) ride out on Celtic Beltaine (May-Eve), to usher in the Summer. The Daoine Sidhe were the Irish version of British fairies, ancient heroes and deities who lived in the Sidhe or 'hollow hills' of the Otherworld. Duncan said that he could hear 'fairy music' as he painted. Duncan gives Celtic authenticity to his late Romantic images: horse-masks and trappings, and cup, sword and shield are all drawn from ancient examples.*

TWO

The Story of Deirdre of The Sorrows

This is one of the most popular stories in the oral tradition, and several versions of it were written down between the ninth and the nineteenth centuries. This is a slight adaptation of a version recorded from a Scottish Gaelic oral source in 1887, and is therefore in a 'folk' rather than a 'literary' style. The earlier Irish accounts gave Conchobar (Connachar) as Deirdre's father — presumably this relationship was considered too incestuous and altered in later versions — and the old prophet was Conchobar's Druid, Cathbad. The lovely Deirdre's Lament is from an early Irish account, and the story incorporates pagan divinities which would have been excized by Christianization. The names here are in their Scottish forms: Ferchar mac Ro, for example, would be Fergus mac Roigh in an Irish version. In the early collections of Celtic literature, this is one of the Three Most Sorrowful Tales of Erin (which also include The Children of Lir and The Children of Turireann). It is an episode (probably an evening session in an elaborated oral recital) from a larger hero-tale and deals with the theme of the outcast. The detail of the intertwining lovers' trees may be compared to other love stories, including a version of Tristan and Isolt. A particularly Celtic feature is the powerful female characterization of the heroine Deirdre, including her wooing of the hero rather than waiting for his advances. Early cultural links between Scotland and Ireland are reflected in the story.

M alcolm Harper and his wife lived in a remote corner of Ireland; they wanted a child dearly. They had made offerings to the fertility goddesses but had little hope of success now that they were approaching old age. Unknown to them, however, their prayers were to be answered. An old man who could see what they could not see visited them with a message from the gods: 'You will have a daughter,' he promised, 'but she will be the cause of more bloodshed than this island has ever witnessed. Three men, all of them heroes, will lose their heads because of this woman, your daughter.'

By the end of the same year, a daughter was born but the mother was not even allowed a glimpse of her. Malcolm took the baby from the house and visited a childless woman who lived in their village. 'You can have the child,' said the father, 'but I want her out of this place, where no other living person will ever set eyes on her.' They travelled for three days until they reached the high mountains. On a mountain peak they dug a hole and covered it with a roof of mud and wood: here the foster-mother and baby girl made their home. Malcolm named his daughter Deirdre and departed.

The first sixteen years of Deirdre's life were spent in this humble bothy, which soon became part of the landscape, a green mound touching the blue sky. She saw no one but her foster-mother, who taught her everything that she knew about the flowers and birds which lived around them in the sunlight and the stars which visited them at night. Deirdre, unsullied by the greed and lusts of others, thus grew into a fair young woman. Indeed she was the fairest in Ireland, and if any man had looked into her face, she would have blushed fiery red. Her keeper, now an old woman, in obedience to Malcom made certain that this would never happen, leaving her in the bothy whenever she ventured into the valley for provisions.

In the white winters, kings and noblemen hunted wild boar and stag on the wooded slopes of the mountains. Deirdre would hear their screaming horns and feel the terror of the deer as it bellowed at the rising moon. Her keeper told her that these were the wild hunters of Cernunnos, who would take this lovely girl from you were they to set eyes on her.'

'And what men are these?' said Deirdre, ever interested in knowing the unknown.

'I will tell you since you ask,' said the hunter. 'Naois, the son of Uisnech, and his brothers, Allen and Arden.'

'What do they look like,' hesitated Deirdre, 'if we were to see them, that is?'

'You could not mistake them,' answered the hunter. 'Their skin is as white as the swan against the ripples of a dark lake, their hair is as black as the raven's wing against the bright

wandering the night sky when the moon was at its brightest. It was on such a night that the moon lost herself behind a mass of black thunderclouds. A hunter lost his dogs and companions, and found shelter from the gale beside the green mound. Cold and exhausted he lay down and was soon fast asleep. In his sleep he dreamed of fairies dancing and making music within the mound.

'Let me in before I die of the cold night,' the hunter cried out.

Deirdre heard his voice above the storm. 'There is someone out there,' she said to her keeper.

'Go back to sleep,' replied the old woman. 'It is the sound of birds who have lost their homes in the wind.'

'You yourself once said that we should give lost creatures a home,' replied Deirdre. 'I am going to let a lost bird in.'

She drew the bolt and the hunter entered. Deirdre, avoiding his steady gaze, led him to a seat beside the hearth and brought him food and clear spring water. It was the old woman who broke the silence: 'You are a lucky man to find shelter on such a night. In return you can keep quiet about what you have seen.'

'A fair enough request for saving my life,' said the hunter, 'but by your two hands and the hands of your father and his father, I know men

sky, they have cheeks like the blood of the brindled red calf, and they can run and leap like deer on the mountain slopes or the salmon in the raging torrent. And Naois is the tallest man in the land of Erin.'

'No more of this,' cried the old woman. 'It is time for you to be gone, and by the sun and the light, I wish that you had not come to this place!'

The hunter left and went straightaway to the court of King Connachar of Ulster to tell him that he had found the fairest girl in Ireland and that he would take him to where she lived.

It was on a May morning, before the birds had started singing and with the dew still heavy on the spring flowers, that the King of Ulster set out with his friends and the hunter to track down Deirdre in her green mound on the mountain. It was a long journey over rocky terrain and soon the spring had gone out of the step of even the youngest among them. As they approached the place the hunter called a halt. 'There is the bothy where dwells the loveliest girl in Erin, but you can complete the journey without me; I have no wish to see the old woman again.'

Connachar and his kinsmen approached the mound and knocked at the door. 'It would take the command of a king', called the old woman from within, 'for me to open the door. So tell me who you are.'

'I am Connachar, King of Ulster.' The old woman opened the door and they all crowded into the bothy.

The king looked at Deirdre and saw the girl of his dreams and felt great love for her; but Deirdre, though she blushed a fiery red at his gaze, did not see the man of her dreams. She was raised onto the shoulders of one of Connachar's heroes and was taken with her foster-mother to the court of Ulster.

Connachar told Deirdre of his great love for her and that he desired her in marriage. To the king's surprise the girl replied: 'Allow me a year and a day, and then ask me again.' 'A year and a day I grant you,' said Connachar, 'but only if you promise that you will indeed be my wife on that day.' Deirdre promised, though her heart remained silent. Connachar was content and surrounded his future wife with noble girls and, realizing that she was uneducated, provided her with a teacher. It was not long before this wild girl of the mountains was transformed into a lady fit for a king: but her heart was not in it.

It was summertime and Deirdre was sitting with her new friends on a hillock behind the castle. It was her favourite place, for from it she could see the distant mountains and imagine the birds and flowers around the old bothy. Into her daydream stepped three men making their way along the dusty track which led to the castle gates. As they passed beneath the hillock Deirdre recognized them from the portraits that the hunter had painted in her mind: these were surely the sons of Uisnech. And Deirdre felt for Naois, the tallest of the three, what Connachar had felt for her. Leaving her attendants behind, she ran down the hill in headlong pursuit of the men.

BELOW **The Turoe Stone, County Galway, Ireland** (c. *first century* BC). *The shape suggests a sacred fertility stone: it is similar to the World-Navel stone in ancient Greek Delphi. The carved decoration with its curvilinear stylized foliage is typical of Irish La Tène art.*

Round tower at Clonmacnois monastic settlement, Ireland (*c. tenth century* AD). *This Christian settlement was vulnerable to Viking boats sailing up the River Shannon: such defensive towers were typical of the early Celtic Christians in Ireland. It was here that the* Book of the Dun Cow, *a rich and early manuscript of Irish myths, was written on the hide of a pet cow.*

Allen and Arden had heard of Deirdre's beauty, and had in mind that their elder brother Naois might take her for his own wife: after all, she was as yet unmarried. It was dusk and they were hurrying to reach Connachar's court before nightfall. Deirdre, whose fleet foot was hindered by her courtly dress and shoes, called out after them in despair: 'Naois, son of Uisnech, how can you go without me?' The hero stopped in his tracks. 'What was that cry so harsh and yet so melodious?' 'It is the sound of the swans on Connachar's lakes. We must be near his castle,' replied the brothers. But Naois the hero recognized the voice of a woman in distress and turned to see Deirdre behind him. Deirdre, knowing her loved one to be the man who stood before her and forgetting her new courtly manners, stepped forward and placed three kisses on Naois' brow and one kiss each for Allen and Arden. Suddenly aware of what she was doing, Deirdre blushed a fiery red, but it was gone as quickly as the aspen quivers by the stream. To Naois she was fairer than the fairest vision.

Realizing the strife that this love would cause between himself and Connachar, his uncle's son, Naois took Deirdre on his shoulders and made his way out of Ulster. The three brothers took Deirdre across the sea to Alba, which some men call Scotland. They built a tower beside Loch Ness and were happy together hunting the deer of the mountain slopes and the salmon of the raging torrent.

The day finally arrived when Deirdre had pledged her hand in marriage to Connachar. The King of Ulster could not believe that the woman he loved so well would not return to honour her promise. She did not come. Connachar decided to avenge himself by taking her from Naois, whom he did not consider to be her rightful husband. Therefore he planned a splendid feast to which all the great kings and nobles of Erin would be invited; his uncle, Ferchar mac Ro, was sent off to Alba to give word of the feast to the sons of Uisnech; 'Tell them', said Connachar, 'that I shall not sleep again if they refuse my invitation.'

Ferchar mac Ro and his three sons sailed to Alba and soon reached the tower by Loch Ness. They were warmly welcomed by Naois who asked Ferchar for the news from Erin. 'A great feast is planned by the King of Ulster,' answered Ferchar, 'and the king has vowed by the forces of earth, heaven and the westward-travelling sun that he will not rest unless the sons of his father's brother Uisnech join the celebrations.'

'We accept Connachar's invitation,' said Naois.

Deirdre could see what the invitation really meant and tried to persuade Naois to remain in Alba. Knowing that words alone would not temper her husband's pride at being invited to such a feast of heroes, Deirdre broke into song:

'I had a dream, O Naois, son
    of Uisnech,
A dream for you to read.
On the warm south wind
    flew three white doves
Soaring over the sea,
Bearing in their beaks what
    every child loves,
Sweet nectar from the
    humble bee.

'I had a dream, O Naois, son
    of Uisnech,
A dream for you to read.
On the warm south wind
    flew three grey hawks
Soaring across the sea,
Bearing in their beaks three
    bloody torques
That meant the earth to me.'

And Naois sang:

'I read only the dreams of the
    fearful night,
In the morning they fade to
    dust, Deirdre,
In the morning they fade
    away.'

'And if we fail to accept the invitation from the great Irish king, we shall be an enemy to Erin forever,' added Naois.

Ferchar mac Ro was unaware of Connachar's grudge, and he pledged: 'If anyone should harm the sons of Uisnech, I, Ferchar, and my three heroic sons will fight to the death to defend you.'

Deirdre's sorrows began on the day they set sail for Erin: standing on the stern of the wooden ship she sang her farewell to Scotland:

'Across the waves I see you,
    Alba,
Slipping away from me,
I cry for your woods and quiet
    lakes
But my place is beside the
    one I love,
My heart is beside my Naois.'

And the sons of Ferchar sang:

'We weigh the anchor, hoist
    the sail,
And make towards the ocean
    deep,
In two days' time, come wind
    and gale,
Onto Erin's white shore we'll
    leap, we'll leap,
Onto Erin's white shore we
    shall leap.'

ABOVE **Celtic bronze torc from Dumfriesshire, Scotland** (c. *first century* AD). *Classical writers tell us that torcs were worn in battle by otherwise naked Celtic warriors. The taut abstract designs are found on many types of object in La Tène art.*

35

When they had arrived in Ireland, Ferchar sent a messenger to tell Connachar that the sons of Uisnech had accepted his invitation to the feast. Connachar was not ready for them, and asked them to wait for a day or two in a house reserved for important guests. That evening, wondering whether Deirdre was still the same fair girl that he had taken a year ago from the bothy, Connachar sent for Gelban Grednach, the Prince of Lochlin: 'Pay a visit to the sons of Uisnech, Gelban, and bring me word as to whether my Deirdre has the same fair skin as when she left Erin. If she has altered, then let the son of Uisnech keep her; but if she is still the woman of my dreams, then I shall have her back by the sword's point and the blade's edge.'

Gelban, known for his charm and cheerfulness, walked down to the house where the sons of Uisnech and Deirdre were lodging with the three sons of Ferchar mac Ro: Daring Drop, Hardy Holly and Fiallan the Fair were their names. He did not bother to knock at the door, but peeped at Deirdre through a hole in the door. Deirdre, conscious of the man's gaze, blushed a fiery red as was her wont. The effect was not lost on Naois who, realizing that a man must be staring at his wife through the peephole, picked up a dice from the gaming table and threw it hard at the small hole: his aim was sure, and cheerful Gelban the Charmer returned to Connachar minus an eye.

'You left the court charming and cheerful as ever, yet you return as cheerless Gelban the Charmless,' said the King of Ulster. 'Well, is my Deirdre as fair as when I last saw her?'

'I lost an eye through gazing at her in admiration,' replied Gelban, 'and would have remained to look at her with my other eye, but pulled myself away from the fair vision in order to report back to you.'

'Is she still so fair?' said Connachar. 'Three hundred of my bravest heroes shall take her from the house, killing those that are with her.'

LEFT **Bronze shield from the River Thames at Battersea, London, England** (c. *first century* AD). *Such fine objects appear to have been deliberately thrown into rivers by Celtic warrior aristocrats as votive offerings to the water gods. The shield has curvilinear La Tène designs which become abstract faces in the central roundel. Colour was provided by applied red glass.*

RIGHT **The Druids: Bringing in the Mistletoe** (*by George Henry and EA Hornel; 1890*). *The late nineteenth century saw attempts at revival of Celtic art and language in Scotland: this was one of the first 'revival' paintings. The ancient literary source for this monthly ritual is Pliny the Elder: he relates that on the sixth day of the moon (seen rising above the hill), the Druids climbed a sacred oak and cut off the mistletoe with a golden sickle (held by the leading figure); two bulls were sacrificed. The Druids wear rediscovered Celtic and Pictish jewellery. A year later the two artists painted* The Star in the East *as a Christian counterpart: Christ's birthday fell at the pagan winter solstice, which is the setting for* The Druids.

'Then become one,' said Dearg, and he pointed his own Druid's wand at Oifa. Immediately her face became demonic and her sharp wings took her away into the air to remain an air-demon until the end of time.

The children of Lir sang their songs of sadness to the clans who dwelt around the Lake of the Red Eye until they felt that the time had come to depart. Fingula sang to the people of Dearg and Lir as they stood on the shores of the lake:

'Fare thee well, Dearg our
     king,
You who have mastered the
     art of the Druids!
And fare thee well, dear
     father of ours,
King Lir of the Hill of the
     White Field!

'We are off to live out our
     final days
Far away from the dwellings
     of men.
We shall swim in the flowing
     tides of the Moyle,
Our feathers all bitter and
     salty.

'Till that day when Deoch
     joins Lairgnen,
Let us fly my brothers who
     once had red cheeks;
From the Lake of the Red Eye
     we travel;
In sorrow we fly from our
     loved ones.'

They flew away, high into the sky and out of sight, and took no rest until they reached the Moyle, the water which lies between Erin and Alba. And the people of Erin were so upset at the departure of the swan-children that a law was made banning the killing of swans.

The children found themselves cold and alone with a great storm brewing. Fingula suggested that they agree on a meeting place in case they lost one another in the tempest. 'Let us gather', said her brothers, 'at the Rock of the Seals.' And the lightning and thunder cracked at their words and the children of Lir were thrown apart on the raging deep. When at last it had died down Fingula sang:

'I wish I had died in the
     waters wild
For my wings have turned to
     ice.
My brothers three, come
     back again
And hide once more beneath
     my wings.
But I know that this can
     never be
Till dead men rise from their
     graves!'

She made her way to the Rock of the Seals and two of her brothers appeared, Conn and Fiachra, their feathers heavy with the salt thrown up by the stormy seas. Fingula cradled them under her wings: 'If only our brother Aod were here with us,' she

BELOW LEFT **Din Lligwy, Anglesey, Wales** (*c. fourth century* AD). *A well-preserved native British settlement from the late Roman period. The old Celtic cultural traditions survived in such remote areas, the circular and rectangular huts contrasting vividly with the contemporary luxurious Roman villas of southern England.*

cried, 'then we would be so happy.' Aod arrived with his head and feathers dry and preened. Fingula tucked him under her breast with Conn and Fiachra under each wing and she sang:

'The magical spells of a
wicked woman
Have sent us into the
northern seas,
Transformed by our
stepmother are we
Into magical forms of swans.

'And now our bath is the
water's edge
In the salty foam of the
breaking waves,
And the only ale we drink at
the feast
Is the salty draught of the
deep blue sea.'

One fine day a troop of gleaming white horses came galloping up and the swan-children recognized the two sons of Dearg. 'The king, our father,' they said, 'and indeed your own father Lir, are alive and well, but they have not been happy since you flew away from the Lake of the Red Eye.' Fingula then sang of their lot:

'There is meat and drink in
the court tonight,
In the court of Lir is
rejoicing.
But what has become of the
children of Lir?
Our beds are our feathers,
Our food is the white sand,
Our wine is the deep blue sea.
Beneath my feathers rest
Fiachra and Conn
Under my wings they sail on
the Moyle,
And beneath my breast lies
Aod dear,
Together we lie in our feather
bed.

The sons of Dearg returned and told of what they had seen and the beautiful song that they had heard.

The flowing waters of the Moyle carried the children of Lir to the Bay of Erris where they remained until the fated day when they were to return to the Hill of the White Field. And there they found everything in a state of desolation; only nettles remained where once stood the high walls of dwellings. Three times they cried out their grief. Then Fingula sang:

'How sad it is for me to see
My father's fallen halls:
Here once were dogs and
hunting hounds,
Here women laughed with
gallant knights,

'Here once was heard the
clash of cups
Of horn and wood in merry
feasts,
Now all I see is desolation
My father long since dead
and gone.

'And we his children have
wandered for years,
And felt the cruel blast of
freezing winds;
But the harshest blow of all
has come:
To return at last to an empty
home.'

The swans then flew to the lovely Isles of the West. At that time the prophecy of Fingula's song had come true: Deoch the Princess of Munster had promised to marry Lairgnen Prince of Connaught. But Deoch would not be wed until her prince had brought her the wonderful swans. Lairgnen found them swimming happily on the Lake of the Birds; he rowed out to them and removed their silver chains. In an instant they became human again, but the boys had aged into bony old men and young Fingula was now a bent and scrawny old woman. They died within the hour and were laid to rest as they had been in life: Fiachra and Conn on either side of Fingula, with Aod at her breast.

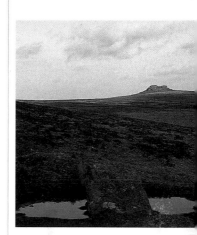

RIGHT **Bronze-Age grave on Shovel Down, Dartmoor, England** (c. *1000* BC). *The upland areas of western Britain provide the best surviving evidence of the Celtic landscape. Here there are Iron-Age farms and field boundaries, outside of which are the stone-circles and burial mounds of the preceding Bronze Age.*

Celtic Storytellers

ABOVE **Beard-pullers and beasts from the Book of Kells** (*Irish; eighth to ninth centuries AD*). *The Christian scribes illustrated their texts with motifs and styles from the pagan Celtic past. The interlacing forms of human and animal figures symbolize the bestiality of man and nature in the eyes of the new religion.*

Our knowledge of the early pagan Celtic poets comes mainly from the recorded observations of their Greek and Roman contemporaries. Diodorus of Sicily, writing in the first century BC, tells us that among the Gallic Celts were 'lyric poets called bards, who accompany their songs with instruments similar to lyres: these songs include praise-poems and satires' (Book V, 31). This suggests that the bards played an important social role: they would be hired to write poems praising their patrons, but also to pour scorn on the patron's enemies.

The bards referred to by Diodorus did not record their poems in writing as did their classical counterparts, but passed them down from teacher to pupil in the manner of prehistoric Greek poetry. And like those early Greek poets, the bard was considered to be a kind of priest, passing religious mysteries on to future generations. This may account for the many 'unexplainable' aspects of the myths. Diodorus tells us in the same passage that they 'converse with few words and in riddles, mainly using obscure hints to refer to things and saying one word when they mean another; and they tend to use superlatives to boost their own achievements and put down those of others.'

The surviving Celtic myths themselves can also tell us about the status of the poets. In the story of the *Dream of Rhonabwy* in the *Mabinogion*, a poet sings a song of praise which can only be understood by other poets. In the medieval period there were highly paid and socially respected bards employed in the houses of the surviving Celtic nobility. There were also wandering minstrels who usually received small payments for their songs, but who certainly helped to keep the oral tradition alive by carrying the poems across Britain and Europe. It was in this period also that the first written versions of the myths were made, although since the scribes were usually monks, the stories were often heavily Christianized.

Finally there were the storytellers, who since time immemorial have told both heroic myths and folk-tales wherever there were people to listen, round the domestic hearth or in a corner of the pub. They still exist in the remoter Celtic areas and their feats of memory are legendary. A fisherman in Barra is recorded as saying that when he was a boy he listened to the same storyteller every night for 15 years and that he hardly ever repeated a story.

The 'high' bardic tradition has survived in the annual Welsh Eisteddfod meetings, but there is also an attempt to revive it in less formal surroundings. The British singer and harpist Robin Williamson performs and records the Celtic hero-tales in spoken and sung poetry to the accompaniment of his 'Celtic' harp and the Breton artist Alan Stivell similarly recreates the Celtic myths of Britanny. The Celtic storytelling tradition is therefore still very much alive for those who wish to experience it.

ABOVE LEFT **Robin Williamson** *The Scottish songwriter and storyteller often accompanies his singing on the Welsh harp. A founder member of the Incredible String Band in the 1960s, more recently he has created sung and spoken versions of Celtic myths and legends. He has also written music and lyrics for a play of the* Mabinogion *and musical accompaniments for a television history of Wales.*

ABOVE RIGHT **A scribe writing a book** *(Anglo-Saxon ivory). Monastic scribes were the only literate men with the time and ability to record the oral Celtic myths in written form.*

FOUR

The Art of Description in Celtic Mythology

Celtic storytellers were experts in the vivid description of imaginary worlds, fantastic animals and superhuman characters. Bright colours and meticulous details of landscape, human appearance and dress are the main characteristics of Celtic descriptive passages, mirroring a similar manifestation of rich colour and detail found in the Celtic visual arts. Descriptions of women tend to be highly voyeuristic and unrealistic, reflecting the male gender of the storyteller, and for the same reason, storytellers glamourized the warrior aspects of their male characters.

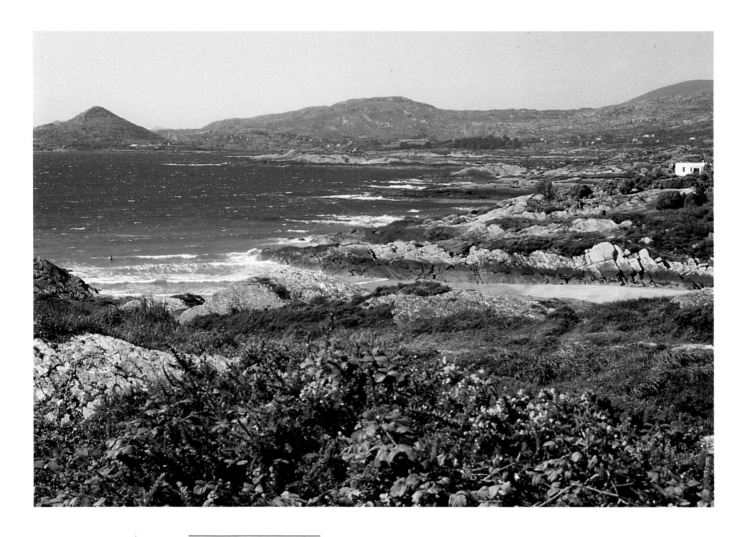

FANTASY LANDSCAPE: THE DISCOVERY OF PARADISE ON EARTH

T he storm was over and the wind blew gently now; the sea-warriors hoisted their sail and the boat took in less water. A stillness fell upon the wide ocean, the waves were smoothed and it was bright and calm. Birds of different kinds never seen before filled the air round about with their singing. A land of graceful shape and fair shores came into view ahead of them; the sailors rejoiced at the sight of it. They sailed closer and entered a beautiful estuary, its green breasts hanging above silver-pebbled beaches, and in the clear waters the splendid deep purple of the handsome salmon flashed; and they looked about them and were pleased by the lovely streams running through woods tinged with purple.

Tadhg the Irish Prince of Munster stood at the bow and addressed his men: 'This is surely the island of our dreams, my fighting men; it is blessed with fruit and all things most lovely; we shall make for the beach, haul up the boat and give it time enough to dry out after its storm-battering.' Twenty stout warriors went on ahead with Tadhg, leaving twenty behind to guard the boat; and the wonder of it was that though they had come through wind and hard rain and the extremes of cold and hunger, they felt no desire for food and the camp fire

ABOVE **The Atlantic coast and the Ring of Kerry mountains, Ireland.** *Mild winters encourage continual vegetation and pasturage throughout the year here; Mediterranean trees grow in some parts. Kerry was on the prehistoric migration and trade routes and has many surviving remains of its ancient past. It is easy to see how such landscapes could be mythologized into paradises.*

ABOVE **Bronze belt hook from the German Tyrol** (*fourth century* BC). *Early La Tène artists preferred running tendril patterns; here 'dragons' (or stylized horses, perhaps?) and human figures are depicted within such a fantasy pattern. Whatever the subject matter, it appears to symbolize the power of man (or god?) over beast, and would therefore have been fitting decoration for the aristocratic warrior.*

the men blink and look again, for they were white birds with purple heads and golden beaks. They sang the songs of minstrels as they ate their fill of the berries, and their music was plaintive and yet so soothing, that it would have lulled wounded warriors to sleep . . .

Anonymous Irish author of the fourteenth or fifteenth century

FANTASY WOMAN: A VISION OF ETAIN THE FAIRY

The men could see a woman beside the spring. In her hand glinted a comb of silver with decorative work in gold and she was about to wash her hair in a bowl of beaten silver with reddish-purple gems glittering on its rim and on its sides four inlaid golden birds could be seen as she turned the bowl. The woman wore the fleece of a fine shaggy sheep dyed purple, and on the shoulders of this cloak were silver brooches worked in twisted filigree with golden ornament. Beneath the cloak she wore, stiff yet smooth, a tunic of green silk with a long hood, embroidered with reddish-gold thread; they could see the interlacing of exotic animals worked into the tunic in gold and silver running over her breasts, shoulders and shoulder blades. The gold gleamed in the sunlight against its green silken background.

Her golden-blond hair was arranged in two long tresses; each tress was made up of four plaits, and at the end of each plait hung a bead. To some men her hair was the colour of the yellow flag iris which grows by summer water; others thought it like ruddy polished gold.

in that place. It was enough and more than enough to breathe in the incense of the trees, glowing with purple flowers about them.

Tadhg led them into the wood beside their path and they soon came to an orchard of glorious purple-fringed apple trees and oaks with leaves of lovely hue and hazels teeming with nuts of bright yellow. 'What a wonderful thing occurs to me,' said Tadhg to his warriors. 'It is winter back home, yet summer reigns here.'

There was indeed no end to the lovely places they discovered in that land. Leaving the orchard, they came upon a wood without shadows, with round purple berries the size of men's heads giving off wonderful scents; and the birds that fed on the berries made flushed now with a purple as red as the blood of the frisky calf and now the white brilliance of snow. Her voice was noble and gentle; she walked as befits a queen, stepping steadily and stately. She was the most perfect woman in the world to behold, as fair and lovely as they could ever hope to see; the men agreed that she must have been a fairy . . .

Anonymous Irish author of the ninth century

She began to untie her hair for washing, her arms reaching out from the openings in her dress. The arms were straight yet soft, their tops as white as a fall of night snow before the sun rises; the skin of her face was clear and her cheeks blushed red like the foxglove on the moor. Like the black beetle's wings were her eyebrows; like a spray of pearls were her teeth; like the brilliant blue starry flowers of borage were her eyes; of bright red vermilion were her lips. Her soft, smooth shoulders stood high and white; of the purest white were her fingers, long and slender as were her arms; and long, slender and soft as pliable wool were her white sides, like the foam on the wavecrest. Smooth, shiny and sleek were her warm white thighs; her small, firm knees were white and rounded; white shins she had, short and straight. She stood straight and even on her heels, which looked lovely from behind; if a straight rule were placed along her feet, no fault would be found, unless the skin or flesh were made to bulge by pressing too hard.

The bright blush of the rising moon glimmered in her noble face; her smooth forehead was high and dignified; the beams of eroticism shone from her royal eyes; her cheeks bore the dimples of her sport which

FANTASY MEN: SOME HEROES FROM THE COURT OF KING ARTHUR

Morfran son of Tegid, was so ugly that he was thought to be an evil demon; therefore he was avoided in Arthur's last battle at Camlan. He was as hairy as a stag. Sandde Angel-Face was also left unharmed at that battle, but for a different reason: he was so beautiful that he was thought to be a heavenly angel.

There were three men, all sons of Erim, best known for their magical speed. Henbeddestr could run faster than any other man, even when they were on horseback; Henwas the Winged could run faster over even the shortest distance than any man or four-footed beast; and Scilti the Nimble-footed was often sent as a messenger by Arthur, for he would

ABOVE **Bronze helmet with decorated neck-guard** *(British; first century* AD*). The Celtic warrior's helmet was often highly decorated depending on his rank. This is a relatively restrained example with decoration in the taut curvilinear La Tène style: however, the holes on the crown might have held a plume or other fixture. Artistic representations of Celtic warriors depict them wearing animal crests, such as birds or boars; horned helmets were also worn.*

said to his wife, 'If there is anything of me in your son, my girl, he will be touched by a magic which removes the warmth from his heart and makes him headstrong. He will have other magical abilities: no one, from in front or behind him, will ever be able to see what he is carrying, however large or small it is; he, more than anyone, will be able to face fire and water; he will be the most loyal page and court official.

Then there was Gwallgoig, who used to keep whole towns awake with his bodily requirements when he was staying overnight: no one could sleep.

Osla of the Great Knife, who carried a short broad weapon at his side, used to be a boon to Arthur whenever he came to a torrent with his army. Osla's knife in its sheath would be placed across the narrowest point above the raging stream so that a bridge was formed broad enough to take the army of the three lands of Britain and its three offshore islands (England, Wales and Scotland, Anglesey, the Isle of Man and the Isle of Wight).

Gilla Stag-Legs was the champion of Ireland at long-jump: three hundred acres were his in one bound.

There were three more great heroes: Sol, who could stand on one foot for a day; Gwaddn Osol, who could level a mountain by standing upon it; and Gwaddn of the Bonfire, a boon to Arthur when his armies encountered woody obstacles: the sparks from his metal-studded soles were as large as pieces of red-hot iron drawn out of the forge.

There were the two great eaters, Hir Erwm and Hir Atrwm. On feasting days they would get their supplies by raiding three hundred towns. Then they would eat till noon and drink into the night; they would not stop eating in bed but would bite off the heads of the rats. When invited to another man's feast they would polish off the meat, be it lean or fat, hot or cold, sweet or sour, fresh or salted. Another eater was Huarwar, son of Halwn, who only smiled when he was

not bother with roads, but take the shortest route, touching the tree-tops and skipping the bog-rushes on the mountain slopes. Scilti was so light of foot that he never once bent or broke the rushes that he stepped on.

Teithi the Elder, son of Gwynham, who barely escaped when his lands were covered by the sea, had come to Arthur's court. Some magic curse was on his knife, so that no haft could be found to fit it; and therefore he lived a life of disease and misery, and died of it.

Drem the son of Dremidydd had eyes that could see the gnat in the rising sun's light as far away as Penn Blathon in Scotland from Cellig Wig in Cornwall.

Cynyr of the Beautiful Beard — some say that Cei was his son — once full. One of the Three Great Plagues of the West Country was caused by his demands to be given his fill from Arthur as a present.

There were a number of curious heroes. Sugn, son of Sugnedudd, had the ability to suck up the sea from beneath as many as three hundred ships, leaving only the dry sea-bed; he used to get red-hot heartburn. Cachamwri, one of Arthur's serving men, could work his way through a barn containing the crops of thirty ploughed fields: he would thresh around with his iron flail until the wooden posts, rafters and cross-beams were lying in as many bits on the floor as there were oats. When Gwefl son of Gwastad had the sulks, his lower lip would hang down to his navel and he would pull the upper lip over his head for a cap. The beard of Uchdryd Cross-Beard was so long that he had to throw its bristly red strands across the fifty rafters of Arthur's hall when he came to visit him.

RIGHT **Neolithic burial cairns in the Loughcrew Hills, County Meath, Ireland** (c. 2500–2000 BC). *Most of the prehistoric graves we see today have had their original earth mounds weathered away. These well-preserved examples allow us to understand the frequent mythological Celtic view of them as 'fairy castles'.*

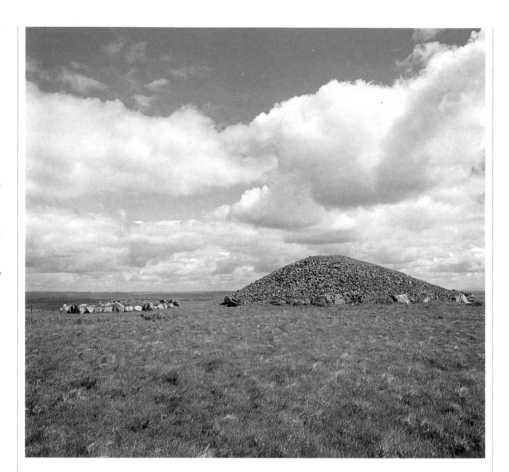

Others had wonderful senses. You could have buried Clust, son of Clust-feinad seven fathoms underground, but he would still have heard an ant getting up in the morning fifty miles away. Medr, son of Medredydd could stand at Celli Wig in Cornwall and shoot through the legs of a wren standing at Esgeir Oerfel in Ireland. Gwiawn, 'Eye of the Cat', could cut the lid from a gnat's eye without damaging the eye.

Cei, whom I have already mentioned, was able to hold his breath underwater for nine days and nine nights; his sword-cut could be cured by no doctor; he could extend his height to look out over trees; his body-heat was such that, when it was pouring with rain, whatever he was holding would stay dry; and when his companions were freezing he was the kindling to light their fire.

Anonymous Welsh author of the tenth century

FAIRY LANDSCAPE: THE WOMAN FROM THE LAND OF EVERLASTING LIFE

Two warriors were walking up on Uisnech: Conn of the Hundred Battles and his red–haired son Connla, one of the Fianna, the hundred and fifty fearless chiefs who led Ireland in the wars. Over the hill came a woman, strikingly dressed so as to make the young Connla exclaim, 'Where did you come from, woman?'

'From Tir Na mBeo, the Lands of the Living,' she replied, 'and not of your world, for there you will find no men looking for a fight, and no one dies. We feast without servants, and bear no grudges. See there,' the woman pointed to a barrow on the ridge. 'That is where we live, and some call us the fairy hill folk.'

'Who is that you're speaking to?' cried Conn, for he could not see the strange woman. She answered for the dumbstruck Connla, 'I am young, beautiful and of high family; and I shall never grow old and die. I have fallen in love with your red–haired son and offer him a place in the court of King Boadhagh, who has known no weeping since he came to power in the Plain of Delights. So are you coming, Connla the Redhead, with the jewels of your torque glinting in your eyes of candle flame? You shall have a crown of gold!'

Conn turned to his Druid, Corann, and said, 'I cannot fight the magic of this woman, for all the battles I have won since I became king. You have the power of song. Use your skills, Corann, against these unseen forces which will take my handsome son from me.' The learned Druid sang his magical song, and no one saw or heard the weird woman as she wandered off, leaving only an apple in her young man's hand.

For a month Connla could not drink or eat, except of his apple; and yet there beside his bed was the apple, untouched. Connla secretly yearned to see the strange woman again.

It happened on the plain of Archommin. He was with his father, who would not let him out of sight, yet she appeared from nowhere, saying: 'I see Connla seated on a high throne, surrounded by the dead, and waiting to join them. Come to the Land of the Living, before it is too late. All the time the immortals are watching you from the hill, waiting for you to join them.'

Conn heard the voice and called for his Druid: 'You have let her evil tongue off the leash, Corann!' 'No!' shouted the woman. 'It is your Druid who is the evil one. One day a good man will step ashore and rid our land of such black magicians.'

Conn saw that his son was being taken in by the woman's words. 'I can't help it!' cried Connla. 'I love my own people dearly, but my longing for this woman overcomes me.'

The woman spoke once more: 'You long to ride the wave of your desire and tear yourself free from your people. In my boat of crystal we might have reached the fairy hill of King Boadhagh. That is now impossible; but look, in the setting sun I can see another land for you. It is far distant, but we can be there by nightfall. All who travel to that land are made happy: only girls and women live there.'

Connla leapt into the crystal boat. Conn and his warriors watched the two rowing into the sunset until their eyes could no longer make them out. They were never seen again.

Anonymous Irish author of the eighth century

ABOVE **Sunset beach at Harlech, Wales.** *In the distance are the hills of the Lleyn Peninsula, some of which bear evidence of Celtic occupation. This area is rich in ancient remains: it was protected by the mountains of Snowdonia from over-exposure to the Romans and later invaders, yet it invited contact with prehistoric Mediterranean and Irish cultures. A perfect setting for the tale of Branwen in the Mabinogion, with its Welsh and Irish topography.*

FIVE

Pwyll, The Prince of Dyfed

The story of Pwyll is the first of the 'Four Branches' (or portions) of the Welsh Mabinogion collection and was probably first written down in the eleventh century. The Mabinogion deals with the birth and childhood of Pryderi, and this self-contained tale based on the hero Pwyll was probably once just the beginning of a complete saga dealing with the life and death of the hero Pryderi.

This relatively late, written version of the myth has lost little of its early pagan quality. The writer was not tempted to alter the powerful simplicity of his characters and reduce them to mythical 'types'. We are immediately plunged into a world where reality and myth intermingle: human characters with earthly passions encounter Otherworld and Underworld characters; one moment we are in a recognizable Welsh landscape, the next we are in a magical country. It is the Celtic storyteller's gift that he can take us in and out of these worlds without us noticing.

The mythological themes include the fathering of an earthly hero by a god; the false slandering of the hero's mother; and the linking of the hero's birth with the birth of a colt (as in the CuChulainn saga). The story is punctuated by hunting, banqueting and love-making, reflecting the preoccupations of the early Celtic chieftains for whom these wonderful tales were composed.

Pwyll ruled the seven cantrefs of Dyfed in the southwestern part of Wales, a land of high sea-cliffs and inland mountains. One day, while he was holding court at Arberth, he felt like going on a hunt in the woods of Glyn Cuch, where the hunting was good. When evening came he set out, stopping the night at Pen Llwyn Diarwya. Before dawn he was up and out with his dogs, loosing them at Glyn Cuch. Pwyll blew on his hunting horn and was off into the woods after his dogs; soon those that were with him were left far behind.

Pwyll followed the yelping of his hounds, but began to hear the cries of another pack mingling with his own. In a few moments he was at the edge of a clearing in the woods, and from the other side of the clearing a stag appeared, chased by the alien pack into the open ground. The hunter's gaze was diverted from the handsome stag to the dogs that brought it down: they were gleaming white in colour, with ears of glowing red. Pwyll entered the clearing and put the strange hounds to flight, so that his own might have their fill of the dead stag.

While all this was happening, the master of the strange hounds approached the clearing on a tall steed; and the horse was dapple-grey and the rider was in hunting clothes of similar hue, a horn hanging from his neck. He rode up to Pwyll and addressed him thus: 'Chieftain of Dyfed, I know who you are, but I refuse to offer my greetings.'

'Maybe your own rank', answered the prince, 'is such as to make that unnecessary.'

'My rank', the stranger answered, 'has nothing to do with it.'

'Chieftain,' said Pwyll, 'then where lies the problem?'

'May the gods hear me,' replied the horseman. 'It lies in your own lack of courtesy and breeding.'

'In what way have I been discourteous towards you, chieftain?'

'Why,' he answered, 'I have never met a man so impolite that he can bait his own hounds on a stag brought to the ground by another man's pack. That shows complete lack of courtesy, and, though I do not seek revenge, I shall make sure that you lose your honour to the tune of a hundred such stags.'

'Chieftain,' replied Pwyll, 'I have wronged you and will win back your favour.'

'How do you mean to do that?' asked the horseman.

'It depends on your rank,' said the prince. 'Tell me who you are.'

'I wear the king's crown in my own land.'

'My greetings then towards you,' said Pwyll, 'but what land is that?'

'My name is Arawn and I am King of the Underworld, which you mortals call Annwn.'

'My Lord,' cried Pwyll, 'then how shall I recover your good favour?'

'In this manner. Another king rules down in Annwn. His name is Hafgan and he makes repeated incursions on my territory. Get rid of him and you will win back my favour.'

'Tell me how,' said Pwyll, 'and I shall gladly do as you bid.'

'You will be joined to me by an oath of friendship,' explained the King of Annwn, 'and I shall disguise you as myself. You will rule in my place in the Underworld, and sleep with the fairest lady imaginable; and neither she nor others of my court will know that it is not me. We shall meet again at this trysting-place in a year and a day.'

I agree to that,' said the prince, 'but how do I find King Hafgan?'

'One year from tonight,' answered the king, 'I have arranged a tryst with him at the ford yonder. You must come to that place looking like me, and you are to hit him with one fatal blow; and however much he entreats you to hit him again, hold yourself back, for if you hit him a second time he will be back fighting me again the next morning.'

'I agree to that,' said Pwyll, 'but what will become of my own kingdom of Dyfed?'

'I shall rule in your stead, and nobody will know the difference between us.'

'Well,' said Pwyll, 'I had better be on my way.'

'I shall be your guide, so that your path will be free of obstacles until we reach my kingdom.' And Arawn and Pwyll descended into Annwn.

'This is my kingdom,' said Arawn, 'and my court is yonder. Go ahead now, all within will recognize you.'

Pwyll walked into the courtyard; on all sides were grand halls and sleeping-quarters; he entered the great hall and was surrrounded by squires who helped him off with his hunting boots. In came two knights who removed his hunting clothes and dressed him in a silken gown brocaded with gold. The hall was soon filled with a throng of handsome people: there were warriors with their pages, all fitted out with the finest armour; and there among them, dressed in a silken gown brocaded with gold was the fairest lady imaginable, the Queen of Annwn. The company washed their hands and sat at table, with the queen and the earl sitting on either side of the Prince of Dyfed.

Pwyll talked with the queen; she was of graceful temperament and the least affected and most eloquent of all the women he had ever spoken with. They wined and dined the evening

ABOVE **Teutonic gilt-bronze brooch from Denmark** (c. 500 AD). *The Teutonic tribes were probably originally close to the Celts of Eastern Europe; by the historical period (the time of the first written records) the two had become separate cultures. Similarities of style and subject matter can be seen in this brooch, with its decorative spirals, frontal wide-eyed faces and monster/human oppositions.*

away to the sounds of minstrels and drinking-songs. Pwyll had never in his life seen such a profusion of fine foods and drinks served in golden bejewelled cups and dishes.

When the time came for bed, Pwyll turned his back on the queen and remained silent until the morning, when they continued to speak with the gentle friendliness of the evening before; and however tender they were to one another by day, every night of the year was as cold as the first.

Pwyll filled this year with the hunt and the feast, enjoying the company and affection of his court, until at last the night arrived for his tryst with the rival king. That man had also remembered the appointment and as King Hafgan approached the ford of Glyn Cuch with his knights, a man on horseback stood on the opposite side of the river and addressed the company: 'Gentlemen, pay attention to what I say. This tryst is between the two men who claim the kingdom of Annwn as their own. The fight is for them alone, and you must stand watch.'

The two kings rode into the ford. Pwyll, King Arawn's substitute, was the first to strike: the blow fell on the central boss of Hafgan's shield which was shattered as was the king's armour behind it. Hafgan was fatally wounded by this single blow and was hanging the length of his arm and spear out of his horse's saddle. 'Chieftain,' he gasped, 'you have no right to kill me; I have not challenged you in any way, and I know no reason why you should wish for my death. But by the gods, now that you have mortally wounded me, put an end to me with a second blow.'

'Chieftain,' replied Pwyll, 'I may come to regret what I have done. You must find another to finish you: I will not do it.'

'Carry me away from this place,' said Hafgan to his knights, 'I can no longer be your king, for my death has at last been accomplished.'

'And gentle knights,' added he

who was acting on behalf of Arawn, 'take my advice and consider whether you are now my vassals.'

'Lord Arawn,' said the knights in unison, 'every man of us shall obey you as the sole king of Annwn.'

'Good,' replied Pwyll, 'I shall receive the submissive, and may the arrogant be humbled by the sword.'

The knights rendered homage to their new king and by noon of the following day the two old kingdoms of Annwn were in one man's power. It was now a year and a day since his first meeting with King Arawn and Pwyll made his way to the tryst at the clearing in Glyn Cuch. Arawn welcomed him: 'I have heard what you have done for me; may the gods reward you for keeping your oath of friendship.'

'Yes indeed,' said the prince, 'and when you return to your own land you will see the proof of what I have done in your name.'

'May the gods reward you,' said the king, 'for what you have accomplished on my behalf.'

ABOVE **Bronze shield-boss from the River Thames at Wandsworth, London, England** (second to first centuries BC). The Celtic La Tène style is evident in this rich votive offering to the water gods by a warrior aristocrat: the taut curvilinear foliate patterns are imperceptibly combined with bird forms. The repoussé designs were hammered from behind the bronze plate; fine details were then engraved onto some of the resulting shapes to give them texture.

RIGHT **Dragon Hill, Uffington, Oxfordshire, England.** *This distinctive hill lies close to the monumental chalk-cut White Horse on the side of the Ridgeway, an ancient track rich in prehistoric and Celtic remains and legends. A legend tells of Saint George killing the dragon on the summit: no grass can grow where its magic blood was spilled, hence the bare chalky patch. Saint George was originally a pagan smith god who also slew dragons: the new religion transformed him into a saintly Christian soldier.*

King Arawn returned the Prince of Dyfed to his proper appearance and took back his own from Pwyll. He rejoiced greatly on his way back to Annwn, for he had missed his warriors and court. They received him with the customary politeness since they were unaware of his absence. Yet the king spent the day in feasting and drinking, and spoke all day and evening to his wife and nobles. Weary of the day's feasting, at last they retired to their beds.

Arawn continued the evening's conversation in bed with his wife and, not having slept with her for a year, made love to her with great passion. She lay awake in the afterglow wondering at his sudden erotic fervour after a year of coldness. 'Why', asked her husband, 'have you gone quiet?'

'Why', she answered, 'do you ask me that after a year of quietness?'

'But', said he, 'we have always been close in bed.'

'I swear', said she, 'that for a year and a day we have neither spoken nor even faced one another in bed.'

That made Arawn think: 'By the gods,' he said to himself, 'my new comrade is an honourable man indeed.' And then he spoke the truth to his wife: 'My lady, do not blame me for what I am about to tell you.' And Arawn recounted his adventures in the Land of the Living. 'May the gods hear me,' said she, 'when I say that you have great influence over your friend for him to resist sensual pleasures and keep his faith.'

Meanwhile Pwyll had returned to his own lands in Dyfed and had made inquiries into what his subjects thought about his government over the past year. 'My lord,' they all replied, 'we have never known you to be so affable, lovable and generous.'

'By the gods,' he said, 'you should be thanking the man who really was with you. A year and a day ago . . .' And Pwyll told them his story. When he had finished his men said, 'Well, my lord, we have the gods to thank for such a friendship; but you will not grudge us the good that has been accomplished this year?'

'By the gods, of course not,' replied the Prince of Dyfed.

From that day onwards the two leaders continued to grow in friendship. They sent one another heartfelt gifts for the hunt: fine falcons, hounds and horses. Pwyll was greatly honoured by the people of Dyfed for what he had achieved during his year in Annwn; indeed, they considered that his bravery in uniting the two realms was such as to deserve a higher title than Prince of Dyfed: from that day onwards Pwyll, Chief of Annwn, was his name.

Some time later Pwyll was at his court at Arberth enjoying a great feast. After the first course, he felt like walking to the top of a mound, called Gorsedd Arberth, which towered up behind the court buildings. One of his courtiers warned him, 'It is said that if a man of noble birth takes his seat on top of the mound of Gorsedd Arberth, he will either come away covered with wounds, or else he will have seen something wonderful.'

'No one can harm me when I have so many of my men around me,' Pwyll replied, 'but I should like to see this wonderful thing.'

Pwyll and his men climbed the mound of Gorsedd Arberth, sat down, and waited. A lady appeared on the road beneath the mound. She rode a large pearly white steed, and was draped in silk brocaded with gold. The horse strode solemnly past the mound and Pwyll addressed his men: 'Do any of you recognize the rider?' None of them answered. 'Then one of you must go and ask her who she is.' One of the men ran down the mound, but at the roadside she had disappeared. He set off after her, but the

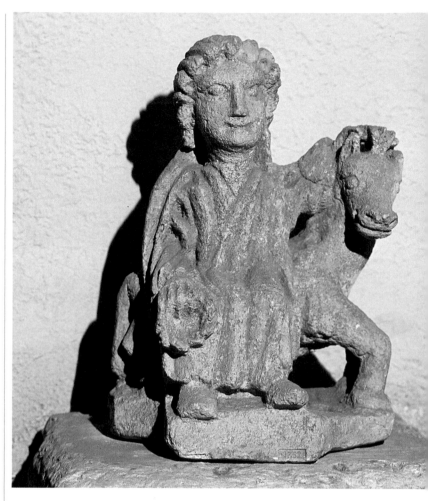

faster he ran the greater the distance between them. He gave up and returned to Pwyll: 'Lord Chief of Annwn,' said the man, 'it is pointless to follow her on foot.' 'Then,' replied Pwyll, 'take the swiftest horse from the stables and catch her up.'

The man galloped away but though his horse was fast and he used his spurs and whip, the lady receded from his view as before. The man returned to Pwyll: 'Lord,' he said, 'there is no faster horse in Dyfed. We waste our time in following after her.' 'Yes,' replied Pwyll, 'magic is the only explanation.'

On the following day they held another feast. After the first course Pwyll once again decided on a walk to the top of Gorsedd Arberth. A swift horse was taken with them. They had just taken their seats on the mound when the lady appeared once more, wearing the same dress and riding the

ABOVE **The goddess Epona on horseback.** *This Celtic deity was the patroness of horses. The Roman cavalry adopted her as their own protective goddess, and this sculpture is carved in a classical style. She may be linked with the mythical Rhiannon in the story of Pwyll: both are Underworld figures. In her right hand she holds what resembles a rose-garland, offered to her by worshippers.*

BELOW **Rhiannon**
(watercolour by Alan
Lee; 1981). Alan Lee's
illustrations for the
Mabinogion combine
Celtic decorative
features with Romantic
medievalist images. A
pervading tone of dark
sepia produces a misty
'Dark Age' atmosphere
in the paintings, which is
broken only occasionally
by the unfading colours
of precious stone jewels,
metals or dyes. This
wonderful mixture of
styles is a perfect visual
counterpart to the
various cultural layers
imposed onto the myths
over the centuries.
Here, Rhiannon
appears as a medieval
Arthurian princess
looking back at her
pursuers. Her birds
were harbingers of the
Otherworld and their
singing at Harlech in the
tale of Branwen
suspends earthly time.

same horse. 'Look there,' cried Pwyll, 'Yesterday's rider. Now one of you, take the horse and go after her!' The lady was just at the foot of the mound riding, as before, at a solemn pace; one of the men started off after her at a moderate canter. But still he could not catch her up, even though he broke into a gallop. Indeed the harder he drove his horse, the further she was from him. He gave up the chase and returned to Pwyll at the mound. 'Lord,' he said, 'you saw how hard I rode.' 'I saw,' answered Pwyll; 'there is no point in trying to catch her. But by the gods, there is some reason for her journey here, if only we could break her resolve to avoid us. Let us all return to the court.'

That night was spent in drinking and singing. On the following day after dinner Pwyll said, 'Everyone who was on the mound with me yesterday is to accompany me there once more.' And he told his stable-groom to saddle his horse and bring his spurs. Up Gorsedd Arberth they went and they sat down. The lady

came into view, in the same silken gold dress and on the same pearly white horse. After her rode Pwyll, but the faster he galloped the further she was from him. Soon he was riding as fast as he had ever ridden in his life, but he saw that he followed her in vain. So he called after her: 'Lady, for the sake of the man you most love, wait for me.'

'I am glad to do so,' she replied, 'and my horse wishes that you had made the request long ago.' She waited for Pwyll and, drawing aside her head-dress, fixed him with her eyes and spoke with him.

'Lady,' asked Pwyll, 'where are you coming from and going to?'

'I go my own way,' she answered, 'and I am pleased to meet you.' Pwyll thought that he had never seen a lady or maiden fairer than the one who was before him.

'Lady,' he asked, 'I would gladly know what you are doing in these parts.'

'Then I shall tell you,' she said; 'it is you I come to see. My name is Rhiannon daughter of Hefeydd the Elder, and he has pledged me in marriage to a man I despise. For my part I will marry no man save yourself. This is the reason for my journey here.' 'My answer to you, by the gods,' said Pwyll, 'is that there is no maiden or lady in the world that I would rather marry.' 'Then let us make a tryst,' she said. 'A year from now at the court of my father Hefeydd a feast shall be prepared for you.' 'I shall be there,' said Pwyll. They went their separate ways and Pwyll changed the subject whenever his men questioned him about her.

A year later Pwyll set off with a hundred men. They rode to Hefeydd's court and were given a great welcome. At dinner Pwyll sat at the top of the table, with Rhiannon and her father on either side of him. They had finished the meat and were beginning their drinking-songs, when a striking young man with reddish-blond hair entered the hall. 'The gods welcome to you,' called out Pwyll to the man, for he looked of royal blood. 'Please be seated.' 'I shall not,' replied the man, 'unless you grant me what I am here for.' 'You shall have what you desire,' said Pwyll. 'Why did you give such an answer?' cried Rhiannon too late. 'He must keep his word,' said the stranger, 'in the presence of such nobles.' 'What is it you want, friend?' asked Pwyll. 'You are feasting,' he replied 'and shall sleep tonight with the lady I most love, and I am here to take your place.'

Pwyll was struck dumb by the stranger's words, and Rhiannon upbraided him for his stupidity: 'This is Gwawl son of Clud, the man who wishes to marry me against my will, and now you must let him have me or you will be dishonoured.' Pwyll did not know what to say. 'You must let him have me,' continued Rhiannon, 'and I shall make sure that he does not have me.'

'How can that be?' asked Pwyll in bewilderment.

'You can remain for the night's feasting, and I shall make a tryst with Gwawl: I shall promise to sleep with him in a year's time, but you are to come to the trysting place with a hundred knights. Leave them in the orchard by the court. Enter the hall in rags and ask him to fill this small bag with food: I shall put a spell on it so that it can never be filled up. When he asks whether it will ever be full, you must answer: 'Only if the greatest in the kingdom presses the food in with his feet.' And when he has his feet in the bag you are to pull it over his head and tie it; then you must blow your hunting-horn as a signal for your hundred riders to take the court.'

'Lord,' interruptd Gwawl, 'I am waiting for your answer.' 'You may take what is in my power to give,' said Pwyll. 'But these men of Dyfed,' added Rhiannon, 'are here as my guests, and they will enjoy the night's feasting. In one year's time I shall

65

66

prepare a feast for you, and then you may sleep with me.' Each chieftain returned to his own court.

When the year was up Gwawl son of Clud came for his feast at Hefeydd's court. Pwyll Chief of Annwn also came, dressed in beggar's clothing as Rhiannon had told him. At the height of the merrymaking, he entered the hall. 'May the gods be good to you and make you prosper,' called out Gwawl. 'The same to you sire,' replied Pwyll, 'and I should like to make a request.' 'So long as it is reasonable,' said Gwawl, 'you shall have what you ask.' 'Will you fill this small bag with food for me to keep the wolves from my door?' 'A humble request,' said he, and he called for the servants to fill the bag to the brim. They could not fill it and Gwawl asked: 'Will the bag ever be full?' 'Only', said Pwyll, 'if the greatest man in the kingdom presses the food in with his feet.' 'Go on then, my man

of valour,' said Rhiannon to Gwawl. And Gwawl had no sooner stepped into the bag than it was up over his head and its thongs were knotted. Pwyll shed his rags and blew his horn. The hundred knights who had hidden in the orchard were soon in the court; as each man entered the hall he smacked the bag and asked, 'What have we here?' 'A badger,' the others cried. And in this manner was first played the game of Badger in the Bag.

Inside the bag Gwawl protested: 'This is no honourable death for me, to be battered to death in a bag.' 'He is right,' added Hefeydd the Elder. 'I accept what you say,' said Pwyll, 'but what must I do with him?' 'This is what you must do,' said Rhiannon. 'The court poets and suitors are now at your command if Gwawl will make them over to you; and you must make him swear that he will not seek revenge for this night's events.' 'I swear,' called Gwawl, and he was let

OPPOSITE **Cross-legged figure on a bucket handle found in the Oseberg ship burial, Norway** (c. ninth century AD). The enamelled, geometric patterns on the figure's chest are typical of late Celtic Irish art, and the bulging almond-eyes and angular features also betray a Celtic origin. The bucket was probably loot from a Viking raid on Ireland. The figure might represent Cernunnos, whose iconography often portrays the hunter god with crossed legs.

LEFT **Late Bronze-Age sacrificial well at Moen, Denmark** (c. 800–400 BC). The stylistic similarities in the art of non-Celtic northern Europe points to cultural connections during the Bronze Age. The well held votive bronze vessels and ornaments as well as animal sacrifices. There were also remains of joints of meat in an alder trunk.

was a great scream from the courtyard and Teyrnon rushed out but could see nothing in the darkness. Remembering that he had left the door open behind him he gave up his pursuit and ran back to his room. In the doorway was a baby boy in swaddling-clothes, wrapped in a gold brocaded silk sheet.

Teyrnon took the boy into his wife's room. 'My lady,' he called, 'are you asleep?' 'I was', she replied 'before you came in.' And Teyrnon told her what had happened in the night and that he had a noble son for her. 'I shall pretend that he is our own child, since we have never had one,' she said. The boy was taken to the holy stone and baptized by a Druid. He was named Gwri of the Golden Hair, for his head was ablaze with gold. By the end of the year Gwri was already walking confidently about the court like a three-year-old. After two years he was more like a boy of six. And before he was four he was already arguing with the stable-hands to let him take their horses to water. Teyrnon's wife recalled the handsome colt that was born on the night the boy appeared and she had it broken in for Gwri to ride.

In the meantime they heard the news concerning Rhiannon and her punishment. Teyrnon Twryf Liant wondered at the story, for it had happened on the same May-eve that the boy had been found. Teyrnon had often been amazed at the striking resemblance between the foundling and Pwyll Chief of Annwn, and he now realized the truth. His wife agreed that their Gwri of the Golden Hair should be sent to Rhiannon: 'We shall gain three things by doing this,' she said. 'Rhiannon's gratitude for releasing her from her punishment; Pwyll's favour for looking after the boy and educating him; and, moreover, should the boy grow into a hero, he shall be our foster-son and do good deeds for us.'

The following day saw Teyrnon and two of his knights riding towards Arberth. Gwri rode beside them on the handsome colt. As they approached the court a woman called to them from the horse-mounting block: 'Let me take you both the rest of your journey on my back, for I killed my son in my sleep with my own hands.' 'None of us will go on your back,' said Teyrnon, 'but we shall walk beside you.'

The hall was filled with sounds of great rejoicing at the homecoming of Rhiannon's son. Pwyll and Rhiannon placed Teyrnon between them at table; on the other side of Pwyll sat Teyrnon's two knights with the boy between them. After dinner the drinking began and each told their own wonderful tale. Teyrnon told of the mare and the foundling boy, and everyone present saw the features of Pwyll in the boy's countenance.

'If this really is my own son,' cried Rhiannon, 'I shall be delivered of my care.' 'This phrase of yours shall be his name,' said Pendaran of Dyfed, 'Pryderi, for that means 'Care' in our Celtic speech!' 'Though Gwri of the Golden Hair is also a fitting name,' said Pwyll, 'it is most fitting that he has the name his mother cried when she heard that he was safe: Pryderi, son of Pwyll Chief of Annwn.' Teyrnon Twryf Liant and his wife were praised by the assembly and Pwyll and Rhiannon offered them gifts of fine horses, hounds and jewels: but Teyrnon Twryf Liant refused them all and went back home content with the praise.

Pwyll and Rhiannon placed Pryderi in the care of the noble Pendaran of Dyfed. Pwyll grew old and died and Pryderi grew into a handsome hero and was loved by the people of the seven cantrefs of Dyfed. His conquests took in the three cantrefs of Ystrad Tywi and the four of Ceredigiawn: these are the seven cantrefs of Seisyllwch. And one day Pryderi son of Pwyll Chief of Annwn married Cifga, daughter of Gwyn Gohoyw, son of Gloyw Wallt Lydan, son of Casnar Wledig: these were sons of the high kings of this island.

Here ends the first branch of the *Mabinogion.*

LEFT **Gold Thracian helmet from Cotofenesti, Romania** (c. 400 BC). *The warrior aristocrats of Thrace, like their Celtic neighbours, wore finely decorated armour of precious metal to display their social status. The cheek-flaps of this unusually rich helmet depict men confronting monsters, a typically Celtic motif signifying power and bravery.*

71

Archeology and Celtic Sites

Ancient writers began to refer to the Celtic civilization from the fifth century BC onwards. These literary accounts by Greek and Roman authors present an external and generally biased view of Celtic society which needs to be balanced by the objective research of modern archeology. Scientific excavation of physical Celtic remains can often tell us more about the Celts than the witness and hearsay of the classical authors. However, because of the lack of Celtic literary sources and the fragmentary nature of the material evidence (there is no Celtic 'Pompeii'), archeological controversies abound. The recent discovery of a peat-preserved man in Lindow Moss, near Manchester, England, has led to various opinions concerning his identity, ranging from executed criminal to murdered aristocrat or Druidic sacrifice. Likewise, opinions vary as to the exact function of Iron-Age hill-forts: were they permanent villages or temporary shelters?

These problems of interpretation were highlighted in the excavation of an archeological site at Hayling Island, Hampshire, England. In 1975–76, excellent weather conditions for the discovery of new archeological remains occurred, as due to drought crops growing over buried walls received less water than usual and became stunted (these variations in height appear as darker areas or 'crop-marks' when seen from above). Aerial photographs of Hayling Island in 1976 revealed a rectangular walled enclosure some 40 sq m/48 sq yd surrounding a circular structure. Early this century archeologists had interpreted the site as a Roman villa with a fish-pond at its centre, a most unusual plan which was further called into question by certain features in the aerial photographs. New excavations were undertaken between 1976 and 1981, and as the modern layer of topsoil was gradually removed and various investigatory trenches were dug, further clues as to the history and function of the site were brought to light.

The circular structure was found to have had two quite different building periods. The earliest had post-holes sunk

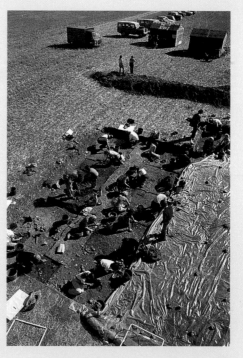

LEFT **Excavating the Hayling Island Celtic temple.** *The site was systematically stripped in order to recover every available piece of evidence, however small: a coin or a fragment of pottery can provide crucial dating and other information, such as of trade patterns. The polythene sheeting sealed moisture in the unexcavated area, so that soil colour variations were retained: these provided pointers to the sub-surface remains.*

OPPOSITE **Aerial photograph of Romano-Celtic temple site, Hayling Island, Hampshire, England in June 1976.** *The rectangular boundary and circular temple were clearly visible as crop-marks during the severe drought of 1976. Many other British sites were revealed by the dry weather that year.*

LEFT **Foundations of the circular temple, Hayling Island.** *The stone foundations of the Roman building can be seen surrounding the gullies of the earlier British structure. The radial sliced wedges are archeological trenches which gradually revealed the various layers of the building's history. The central pit was possibly for holding a ritual stone or sacred wooden post or 'totem pole'.*

LEFT **Bent spear from the Hayling Island site.** *The rectangular courtyard contained votive burials of intentionally damaged military equipment, including spearheads, swords and chariot equipment. These suggest that the cult activity was in honour of a warrior god. Pig and sheep bones provided evidence of animal sacrifice.*

ABOVE
Reconstruction drawing of the Celtic temple and sacred enclosure, Hayling Island. *In the first century* BC *the sanctuary appears to have been a fairly temporary structure of wood and thatch. Most of the votive offerings were found around this earlier structure.*

into an inner circular gully with two larger post-holes at the entrance suggesting that the original building was a typical Celtic 'roundhouse' dwelling, probably roofed with thatch and with a doorway on its eastern side. However, excavations in the surrounding courtyard revealed the true function and approximate date of this early structure. The finds included votive offerings often grouped around burnt areas: sheep and pig bones; Celtic coins (dating the first building and subsequent ritual activity to around 50 BC onwards); horse equipment; and weapons.

All this material evidence suggested that the 'roundhouse' was actually a Celtic temple, typically orientated towards the rising sun, in use during the period of early Roman contact. Contemporary literary sources help to explain the wider context of the discoveries. Julius Caesar tells us (*Gallic War*, Book VI, 17) that the Celtic Gauls used to bring piles of booty from the battlefield to their sacred places, where they would dedicate them to a war god and accompany the ritual with animal sacrifice. Among the Hayling Island votive weapons were spearheads, intentionally bent during the rituals to signify the defeated enemy. The sanctuary was in a region of Celtic inter-tribal warfare until the Roman invasion, so there was ample opportunity for such military victory dedications.

Far from being destroyed after the Roman invasion in AD 43, this potent architectural symbol of Celtic religion was added to; a second building was put up by the Romans soon after the Claudian invasion. It was a larger and more permanent stone version of the Celtic temple, and apparently even more imposing. The width and depth of the surviving foundations suggest a high tower surrounded, like many other Romano-Celtic temples, by a covered portico. Roof tiles and eye-catching red wall-plaster were found which would have covered the temple's exterior, and an entrance porch had been built. There was no evidence to identify the deity, but a similar site in Gaul included an inscription to the Romano-Celtic war god, Mars Mullo.

It is interesting that there were far fewer votive offerings from the Roman period, suggesting that the site was now intended as a symbol of the dominant Romano-Celtic culture rather than as a place for native British religious ritual. This important evidence from Hayling Island not only confirms Celtic religious architecture and ritual, but also indicates the apparent continuation of Celtic religious activity during Roman domination.

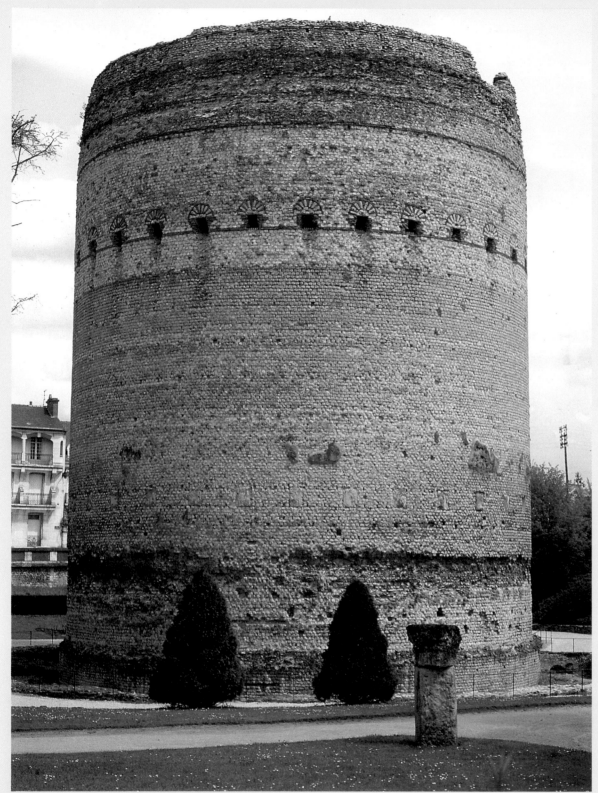

OPPOSITE
Reconstruction drawing of the Romano-Celtic temple and sacred enclosure, Hayling Island. *After the Roman invasion of southern Britain in* AD 43, *the temple and sanctuary were rebuilt in more durable materials. The new buildings were larger and more impressive, but the ritual activities around the temple virtually ceased.*

OPPOSITE BELOW
Reconstructing Iron-Age huts at Butser Hill, Hampshire, England. *Archeology has provided evidence of sizes, shapes and materials used in building Celtic dwellings. The original Hayling Island temple probably looked like one of these roundhouses. Butser Ancient Farm has also launched experiments with Celtic farm animals, crops, cooking and pottery methods.*

LEFT **Temple of Vesunna (?), Perigueux, Dordogne, France** *(late first to third centuries* AD*). This rare survival of a Romano-Celtic temple gives some idea of the probable appearance of the second Hayling Island temple. The Gallic building was originally 24 metres (79 ft) high and (unlike Hayling Island) had an ambulatory: the holes for its roof beams can be seen 11 metres (36 ft) up. It too was orientated eastwards and had a larger galleried portico.*

SIX

The Story of Branwen, Daughter of Llŷr

This is the second of the 'Four Branches' of the Mabinogion. It hardly mentions Pryderi, and the oral tradition has evidently ousted the original 'childhood exploits' of Pryderi which would be expected in this part of his saga, and has replaced them with the exploits of the children of Llŷr. The Irish settings and mythical themes (the cauldron and the house built for Bendigeidfran for example) would suggest that an Irish storyteller intruded on the original Welsh saga of Pryderi at some stage of the oral tradition.

The grandfather of the children of Llŷr is named as Beli and probably refers to the god Belinus, a Celtic solar deity and legendary King of Britain. The mythological theme of the 'falsely slandered wife' (as with Rhiannon in the tale of Pwyll) recurs in this story. Here it is used as the trigger for revenge and war, reminding the reader of the Greek legend of Helen and the Trojan war. The 'iron-house' in which the giants are nearly killed reflects the pagan Celtic Iron-Age origin of the story, and while some scholars have suggested that it is a mythical version of human sacrifices practised by the Celts, others see it as the kiln used by the enamellers of Celtic jewellery. The Celtic religious notion of water as a supernatural dwelling is present here, seen in the lake from which the giants emerge.

RIGHT **The coast at Harlech, Wales.** *This west-facing stretch of the north-west coast of Wales provides the ideal setting for the tale of Branwen: shallow beaches provided landing-places for ancient ships, while the mountainous hinterland encouraged the building of strongholds, from prehistoric camps to medieval castles.*

The two sons of Llŷr, Bendigeidfran and Manawydan, were sitting on the rock of Harddlech (Harlech) which towers above the Irish Sea. Bendigeidfran was king of the Island of Britain and was staying at one of his courts at Harddlech in Ardudwy, on the north-west coast of Wales below the high mountains of Snowdonia. Beside them on the rock sat the two sons of Euroswydd, Nisien and Efnisien: the four men had the same mother, Penarddun, daughter of Beli, son of Mynogan. And when the sons of Llŷr were angry with one another, Nisien would be their peace-maker, but when they were on the best of terms, Efnisien would be sure to make trouble.

From the rock they saw thirteen ships come sailing from the south of Ireland; the wind was behind them and they approached the Welsh coast with great speed. 'Those ships', said King Bendigeidfran, 'are making for our shores. Let every man in the court arm himself and run down to discover their intentions.' The men went down to the beach and saw that the ships were finely fitted out with beautiful flags of brocaded silk. One of the ships moved ahead of the rest and they saw a shield held up above the deck with its point to the sky as a symbol of peaceful intent.

Small boats brought some of the strangers towards the rock where the king was seated. 'May the gods make you prosper,' he called from above. 'You are welcome. But tell me, who commands these ships?'

'My Lord,' they shouted back, 'they belong to the King of Ireland, Matholwch, and he is here with us.'

'Does he want to come ashore?' said Bendigeidfran.

'Not unless he succeeds in his mission,' answered the Irishmen.

'And what mission is that?' asked Bendigeidfran.

'My lord, our king would be your ally; he asks for the hand of your sister Branwen in marriage and thus to form a mighty union between Ireland and the Island of the Powerful.'

'Well, bring him ashore then,' said Bendigeidfran, 'and we shall discuss the matter.'

The Irish king and his men came ashore and made welcome that evening at the crowded court. The next morning Branwen was promised to Matholwch: she was one of the Three Matriarchs of the island, and the most beautiful woman in the world. It was decided that they should all journey to Aberffraw, Matholwch with his ships and Bendigeidfran by land; there the Irish king would sleep with the daughter of King Llŷr.

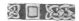

They all met at Aberffraw and entered a great tent for the feast, for Bendigeidfran was too large for any house. On either side of the King of the Island of the Powerful sat his brother Manawydan, son of Llŷr, and Matholwch; and next to the King of Ireland sat Branwen, the daughter of Llŷr. And when they had tired of talking, drinking and singing, they went to bed and Matholwch slept with Branwen.

Matholwch heard the news from his men. 'Your property', said one, 'has been harmed and harm will come to yourself.'

'But why', said Matholwch 'should they wish to do this to me when they have just given me such a lady of high rank and beauty?'

'Whatever the cause,' said another, 'the effects are plain to see. You must return to your ships.' And so the King of Ireland prepared to sail back to his own land.

ABOVE **The Gundestrup Cauldron, Denmark** (*first century* BC). *On this silver inner panel of the gilt-silver ritual vessel, the artist depicted warriors going into battle, preceded by a ram-horned snake. The figures on the right blow carnyxes, or war-trumpets; some of the warriors have bird and boar crests, or horns, on their helmets; on the left, a god dips a human sacrifice into a bucket.*

On the next day the men of Ireland were given billets for their horses and grooms on the land between the court and the sea. Efnisien, the troublemaking half-brother of Bendigeidfran, saw the billets and asked whom the horses belonged to. 'Why,' said the grooms, 'these are Matholwch, the King of Ireland's horses.'

'Will you tell me, then,' asked Efnisien, 'what they are doing here?'

'Why, our Irish king is on a visit to sleep with your sister Branwen, and the horses are his.'

'How dare they do such a thing to my sister without first asking me,' said Efnisien. 'I have never been so insulted in my whole life.' And he cut the horses' lips back to their teeth, their ears to their heads, their tails to their backs, and when he managed to catch hold of their eyelids he tore them from the bone. The horses were maimed beyond repair.

LEFT **Iberian bronze female figurine, from Aust-on-Severn, Gloucestershire, England** (*c. fourth to third centuries* BC). *Similar objects are known to have been made in Spain. The glass-eyed figure was probably imported from Iberia along the trade-routes of the Atlantic coast.*

When Bendigeidfran discovered that his royal guest was making ready to leave the court without giving polite notice, he sent messengers after him to question his motive. 'Is that not obvious?' replied Matholwch. 'I am amazed to have first been offered Branwen, the royal daughter of Llŷr who is, after all, one of the Three Matriarchs of the Island of Britain, and then to have received such outrageous insults as these.'

'No man in the court of Bendigeidfran committed this act, at least not with his authority.'

'I wish I might believe you,' said Matholwch, 'but the insult stands.'

The messengers reported Matholwch's words to Bendigeidfran. 'We must not allow him to leave in anger,' said the king. 'Brother Manawydan, take messengers and offer him the finest replacements for his injured horses; take him also this silver staff and golden plate and tell him that I know that my half-brother committed this crime, and that it would be difficult to punish him with death. Let him come and discuss peace on his own terms.'

Matholwch and his men accepted the offer and that night another great feast was prepared in a tent as before. Bendigeidfran noticed the change of heart in his new ally and decided to improve his peace-offerings: 'You are to have a cauldron of magical strength: for if one of your men is killed, and you throw him into the cauldron that evening, by the morning he will have revived to perfect health except that he will have lost the power of speech.' And Matholwch was exceedingly pleased with the new gift.

The next day Matholwch received new horses from the surrounding territories and once more they sat together at dinner. 'Tell me,' said Matholwch, 'how did this cauldron come into your possession?'

'Well,' replied Bendigeidfran, 'it was brought to me from Ireland by Llasar Llaes Gyfnewid and his wife Cymidei Cymeinfoll. You must know

the story of how they fled from the white-hot House of Iron, for this escapade took place in your own island.'

'Yes, lord,' said Matholwch, 'and I can complete it for you. One day I was out hunting on a mound which overlooks the Lake of the Cauldron. I saw a reddish-blond man emerging from the lake carrying a cauldron; he was huge and monstrous and was accompanied by a woman twice the

size of him. They came towards me and I greeted them. The man addressed me, saying, "This woman is going to conceive a son at the end of a month and a fortnight, and the son will be born fully armed and ready for battle." I took the pair of them into my care. For a year they behaved themselves, but the following year they began to cause disturbances in the land, molesting both ladies and gentlemen. Soon everyone hated them and a petition was raised for me to destroy the pair. This was not easy because both of them were so huge and strong. Therefore blacksmiths came from all over Ireland and built an iron house. The monstrous pair were tempted in with plenty of food and drink. And when they were drunk a great fire was lit around the house of iron, but they escaped through the wall with a mighty shoulder-charge. Presumably they then came across the sea to you with the cauldron?'

ABOVE **The Gundestrup Cauldron, Denmark** *(first century* BC*). This interior silver panel represents a divinity and warrior grappling with a wheel. The wheel is a solar symbol in Celtic art, and it is interesting that griffins are also depicted as these were Greek monsters associated with the sun-god Apollo. The Celtic god could be any one of a number of sky divinities.*

CELTIC MYTHOLOGY

BELOW **Gilt-silver brooch from Ardagh, County Limerick, Ireland** (c. *eighth century* AD). *The meticulous golden filigree and granular decoration of this late Celtic penannular brooch would have signified a high degree of wealth and social status in the wearer.*

'No,' said Bendigeidfran, 'I shall tell you how the cauldron came to me. I allowed the pair to go where they please on my island, for wherever they went they built grand fortresses for my warriors.'

It was a feast of great joyfulness, and the kings talked well into the night. The following day Matholwch set out with Branwen for Ireland; they sailed from Aber Menei in their thirteen ships. There was much rejoicing in Ireland at their return, and every noble man and lady who visited the king brought Branwen some lovely brooch or ring or perhaps a royal jewel from their own treasure. Branwen was a favourite with everyone, and that year she bore a son who was named Gwern, son of Matholwch. He was sent away for a fine education.

But as it became known how Matholwch had been insulted during his visit to Wales, there was a change of spirit in Ireland. Soon even those close to him were demanding revenge and Branwen was forcibly put in the kitchens to cook for the court, and to have her ears boxed daily by the butcher when he had finished with the meat. 'And you must refuse permission', added his men, 'to any ship wishing to travel to Wales. And likewise you must take prisoner any who come from there.'

Meanwhile, Branwen trained a starling and taught it to speak so that it might talk of the insults she was suffering in Ireland. She tied a letter under its wings and sent it off across the sea to her home, where at last it found Bendigeidfran at his court of Caer Seint in Arfon. It landed on his shoulder and spread its wings so that all might see the letter. They realized that the bird was tame and the letter was read aloud to the court. When Bendigeidfran learnt of his sister Branwen's unhappiness he gathered a great army from the whole island and they decided to make war on Ireland. Seven lords were left behind at Edeirnon to guard the realm, and for this reason the town became known as Seith Marchawg ('Seven Riders'). The chief of them was Cradawg, son of Brân.

Bendigeidfran set off with the gathered armies of Britain and he himself waded across the sea, for in those times the water was deep but not wide. On the hills above the coast of Ireland the swineherds saw a marvellous sight and came to tell Matholwch: 'We have seen marvels today,' they said, 'for across the sea we have seen a forest and beside it a mountain, where there was neither forest nor mountain before; and what is more, they are moving towards Ireland.'

Matholwch was baffled by the report and sent messengers to ask Branwen if she could explain the phenomenon. 'I am no lady as you call me,' she replied, 'but I know what this marvel is. The forest is a fleet of ships and the mountain is my brother Bendigeidfran, for he will come by wading as there is no ship big enough to hold him.'

'But,' said the men, 'we also saw a ridge on the mountain with two lakes on either side.'

'My brother's angry eyes on either side of his nose,' laughed Branwen.

Matholwch called on all the armies of Ireland to come and take counsel, and they decided to retreat across the River Llinon (Shannon or Liffey) and break down its bridge, for the river was full of rocks which would obstruct the British boats.

ABOVE **Branwen**
(watercolour by Alan
Lee; 1981). Branwen
sends her starling to
Wales bearing the
message of her
dishonour at the hands
of the Irish. On the
frame, Alan Lee has
depicted the Welsh fleet
sailing across the Irish
Sea; the eyes and arms
of Bendigeidfran can be
seen above and to the
sides of the main
painting.

geidfran and his men and the other half is for yourself and all of us.'

Bendigeidfran accepted the offer on Branwen's advice. The house was indeed built, but the men of Ireland had planned a trick. On all the pillars of the house they fixed pegs, and from every peg was hung a sack, and in every sack they hid an armed warrior. Efnisien entered the house and immediately questioned one of the Irish as to the contents of the bags: 'What is in this one?' he asked and squeezed it hard. 'Only flour, friend,' answered the Irishman. Efnisien asked the same question and received the same answer of all two hundred bags; he squeezed one so hard that the man inside was crushed to death.

The men of both islands entered the hall and Gwern, son of Branwen, was invested as the new king. He greeted Bendigeidfran and Manawy-

Bendigeidfran and his fleet arrived at the river. 'How can we cross over this river?' asked his men. 'There is no bridge,' answered Bendigeidfran, 'so I as your chief shall be a bridge for you.' (That was the first saying of this well-known proverb.) He lay across the river and the armies passed across him.

The Irish armies sent messengers to offer the kingdom of Ireland to Branwen's boy Gwern, son of Matholwch: 'This is to repair the wrong that Matholwch has committed to you and your sister,' said the messengers. 'It is up to you to decide what will become of Matholwch.'

'I am rather inclined to become King of Ireland myself,' answered Bendigeidfran, 'unless you come up with better terms than that.'

The messengers returned to Matholwch and told him to think of a better offer. 'What do you all suggest?' said Matholwch.

'Well,' they replied, 'he has never been able to find a house large enough to hold his great body. So we suggest that you have such a house built, and that half of it should contain Bendi-

ABOVE **Clapper bridge over the Waller Brook, Dartmoor, England.** *These primitive bridges are believed to date back to the Saxon period. The area is rich in Bronze- and Iron-Age settlements and the Celts would also have had to cross these streams; their bridges were probably of wood.*

dan, the sons of Llŷr; Nisien, son of Euroswydd called him over, and the boy went as a willing friend. But he would not approach Efnisien. 'Why does the boy avoid me?' said Efnisien; 'after all, I am his uncle.' Bendigeidfran sent him across to Efnisien, who cried: 'May the gods witness the atrocity I am about to commit.' And he took hold of the new boy king and threw him head-first into the great fire. When she saw her dying son, Branwen in her despair tried to jump into the fire with him, but her brother Bendigeidfran held her back, protecting her with his shield in the fight that followed.

Many warriors died that night. The Irish took the magic cauldron and built a fire beneath it, casting their dead into it until it was full: the next morning they would be as good as new, save that their power of speech would be gone forever. Efnisien realized that the cauldron was not for the dead of the Island of the Mighty: 'May the gods hear me in my distress,' he cried, 'for I have led so many of my countrymen to their deaths. I shall win back my honour and redeem the Island of the Mighty from defeat.' He lay down unseen among the Irish dead and was thrown into the cauldron by two survivors.

Once inside he pushed hard against the sides of the cauldron: it broke in four pieces and his heart burst with it.

Efnisien's deed brought but small assistance to the Island of the Mighty. Bendigeidfran's foot had been wounded by a poisoned spear and only seven of his men survived: these were Manawydan; Pryderi; Glifieu, son of Taran; Taliesin; Ynawg; Gruddieu, son of Muriel; and Heilyn, son of Gwyn the Old.

Bendigeidfran ordered his men to cut off his head: 'Take it to the White Mount in London,' he said, 'and bury it there facing France. Your journey will take some time. Rest at Harddlech for seven years of feasting; the birds of Rhiannon will sing to you and my head shall be as good company as it was when it sat on my shoulders. Your next resting place will be for eighty years at Gwales in Penfro. The sign for departure will be the opening of the door which looks across Aber Henfelen towards Cornwall; from that moment you must not rest until my head is buried in London. Now cross the sea to Wales.'

His head was cut off and the seven crossed over to the other side, Branwen and the head of Bendigeidfran with them. They landed at Aber Alaw in Talebolion. Branwen looked back across the sea to Ireland and at her own Island of the Mighty. 'Pity that I was ever born,' she cried, 'for I am the cause of the destruction of these two fine islands!' She sighed to the heavens and her heart was broken. She was buried by her companions in a four-sided tomb on the banks of the River Alaw.

The seven men carried the head to Harddlech. On the road they met a group of travellers. 'Any news?' asked Manawydan.

'None,' they replied, 'except that Caswallawn, son of Beli, has conquered the Island of the Mighty and now wears the crown in London.'

'Then what has happened to the seven men we left behind as guardians under the leadership of Cradawg, son of Brân?'

'Six of the men were killed by a sword without an owner: Caswallawn held the sword, but wore a magic cloak to make him invisible. Caswallawn would not kill his nephew Cradawg, but his heart was broken by what he saw. Cradawg became one of the 'three men whose hearts were broken by despair'. One young man, Pendaran Dyfed, fled into the woods.'

They reached Harddlech where they feasted for seven years. While they were eating and drinking, three birds sang them a song lovelier than any they had ever heard; and though the birds hovered far out to sea, their song was clear within the hall.

After seven years they made for Gwales in Penfro, where they were entertained in a fine royal castle which towered above the sea. The hall had three doors, two of which stood open. 'We must not open the third door,' said Manawydan, 'for it looks towards Cornwall.' The eighty

LEFT **Bull-headed terminal of iron firedog, Capel Garmon, Denbigh, Wales** (c. *first century* BC). *One of a pair used to support roasting spits over a fire, the bull was a Celtic symbol of virility and would have been a fitting decoration at a warrior banquet.*

RIGHT **Wooden figure
from Ralagan,
County Cavan,
Ireland** (c. *first century*
BC). *Before they learnt
stone-carving techniques
from the Greeks and
Romans, the Celts used
carved wooden images
as representations of
deities and/or
worshippers. This male
figure originally had an
attached phallus and
may have been a fertility
god.*

years were spent without cares in joyful feasting, for they did not age and the head of Bendigeidfran was as cheerful as it had been in life. This feasting was called the Gathering of the Wondrous Head. The earlier feasting in Ireland was called the Gathering of Branwen and Matholwch.

One day, when the eighty years were up, Heilyn, son of Gwyn opened the third door and the company looked out across Aber Henfelen towards Cornwall. The memory of the loved ones lost in battles came flooding back and they mourned the loss of their chief Bendigeidfran. From that moment they did not rest until the head was safely buried on the White Mount of London. That deed was one of the Three Happy Hidings, although one day it would become one of the Three Unhappy Findings, for no plague could cross the sea until the head was found.

This ends the adventures of the men who travelled from Ireland, but those who stayed in Ireland fared worse. No one survived the battle except five women who were hidden in a cave deep in the wild countryside. Each woman carried a son inside her, and when those five sons were born, they grew into fine youths with a desire for marriage. Each son married one of the five mothers, and the land was divided into five and ruled by each. This is how the five provinces of Ireland came into being. They returned to the sites of the earlier battles and found plenty of gold and silver, enough to make them very rich.

Here ends this branch of the *Mabinogion*: we have heard of the insult to Branwen, one of the Three Unhappy Blows on the Island of the Mighty; and of the Gathering of Bendigeidfran, when the armies of one hundred and fifty-four districts crossed the sea to Ireland to avenge the insult to Branwen; we have heard of the seven years feasting at Harddlech and the songbirds of Rhiannon; and we have heard of the eighty-year Gathering of the Wondrous Head.

The Arthurian Legends

In general, the kings, queens and heroes of the Celtic myths are not otherwise known in history, although exceptions occur in the Welsh *Mabinogion*. Cassivellaunus, for example, appears in history as the Belgic chieftain who led the defence of Celtic Britain during Julius Caesar's second Roman invasion in 54 BC: in myth he becomes Caswallawn, the King of Britain, in the tale of *Branwen*. The tendency for myth to ignore the historical realities of time and space can be seen in the placing of Caswallawn in London, which was founded over 100 years after Cassivellaunus fought Caesar. Such inconsistencies between fact and fiction are unavoidable when real men and women become legendary heroes and heroines, and nowhere is this more apparent than in the Arthurian legends.

The earliest mythical tales of King Arthur and his court to appear were probably written in Welsh in the tenth century: the story of *Culhwch and Olwen* is certainly one of the first. In that story we are presented with a pagan Celtic world with quite different social codes to the later Arthurian legends. The poems of the twelfth-century writer Chrétien de Troyes provide the earliest versions of Arthurian romance – the polished medieval conventions of courtly love are epitomized in Lancelot's love for Queen Guinevere; brash warriors of Celtic tradition are transformed into handsome knights; and heroic quests for elusive Druidic tokens become Christian pilgrimages in search of the Holy Grail. Many other medieval Arthurian romances followed and the tales of King Arthur and his Knights of the Round Table were soon well known throughout Europe. Gradually, these loosely connected stories were bound together into 'complete' versions as the quests of various knights were woven around the central heroic figure of Arthur himself, and what were originally non-Arthurian romances, such as *Tristan and Isolt*, were also incorporated.

The late medieval popularity of the Arthurian legends is demonstrated by the fact that Sir Thomas Malory's prose version, *Le Morte d'Arthur* (1485), was one of the earliest

LEFT **Merlin as a stag**
(*medieval manuscript;
Bodleian Library,
Oxford, England*).
*Merlin had the Celtic
sage's ability to shape-
shift. The
transformation into a
stag is in the pagan
tradition of horned
warriors and gods such
as Cernunnos: the stag
signified powerful
animal strength.*

RIGHT **King Arthur
riding a goat** (*mosaic
from Otranto
Cathedral, Italy; twelfth
century*). *The British
hero is found in
medieval art from all
over Europe. Here he is
identified in Latin as
'Rex Arturus' in a
southern Italian mosaic
which incorporates both
biblical and pagan
figures.*

ABOVE **The Failure of Sir Gawaine** (*Edward Burne-Jones [1833–1898]; wool and silk woven on cotton warp, 1895–6*). *Burne-Jones was influenced both thematically and stylistically by the medievalism of the Victorian Pre-Raphaelites, of which he was a late member. In the last decade of his life his interest in Malory* *was revived and he created a series of tapestry designs for his industrialist patrons on the Grail theme. Here Sir Gawaine and Sir Uwain are refused entrance to the Chapel of the Holy Grail because of their sinful natures. The treatment of space and natural detail is intentionally medieval.*

printed works in English. The mythical Arthur fell from favour during the seventeenth century and the Age of Reason, however, but late eighteenth- and nineteenth-century Romantic writers of both prose and poetry revived the medieval Arthurian romances, culminating in the Victorian period with Lord Alfred Tennyson's poem, *Idylls of the King*. The music world also explored the romances; the German composer Wagner found large audiences for his Romantic Arthurian operas *Lohengrin*, *Parsifal* and *Tristan and Isolde*. The twentieth century has kept the tradition alive in music, film, art and literature with novels by TH White, Rosemary Sutcliffe, Mary Stewart and Alan

Garner being just a few of the many works which have dealt with the Arthurian legends, directly or indirectly.

The 'real' historical Arthur has been almost entirely transformed by the romantic legends of the medieval and modern periods. Early accounts of the man, as found in the ninth-century *History of the Britons* and the twelfth-century Geoffrey of Monmouth's *History of the Kings of Britain*, are dubious since their historical 'facts' are extremely questionable. However, cautious use of these sources together with the mythical 'evidence' point to a famous Celtic Romano-British warrior, fighting for a Britain left defence-less by the departure of the Roman legions in the early fifth century. Arthur's enemies probably included the Celtic Picts and Scots, but his major battles would seem to have been against the non-Celtic Anglo-Saxons. The mythical hero-worship in court poetry and folklore of such a patriotic figurehead would have been compounded by the lack of contemporary written literature.

Geoffrey of Monmouth's 'mythical history' began in earnest the tradition of associating episodes from the Arthurian legend with real topographical locations. The most famous of these is Tintagel Castle in Cornwall, which since medieval times has been referred to as the legendary birthplace of Arthur. The highly dramatic setting must have inspired early medieval romantic interpretations, and in return the legendary associations with ancient kings would have encouraged the building of the thirteenth-century castle by the earls of Cornwall. More recently, 'Merlin's Cave' at Tintagel was named after the Arthurian magician for the benefit of late nineteenth-century tourism, and a Victorian lead-mining tunnel became 'King Arthur's Mine'.

Until recently, Tintagel 'island' was believed to have been a monastery, lacking any signs of possible Arthurian connections. But a fire in the 1980s revealed further features and finds which showed it to have been an important community in the late Roman period. More excitingly from the Arthurian point of view, the site appears to have developed into a powerful post-Roman stronghold and centre of trade in the fifth and sixth centuries. However, a separate medieval folk tradition presented Tintagel as the palace of the legendary King Mark of Cornwall with its Tristan and Isolt associations. Such is the power of myth and legend to impose itself on landscapes.

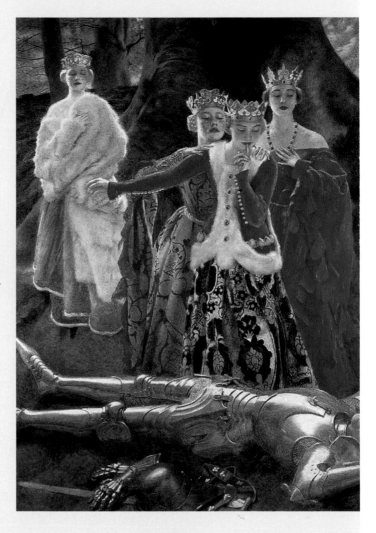

ABOVE **The Four Queens Find Lancelot Sleeping** (*Frank Cadogan Cowper [1877–1958]; oil on canvas, 1954). Cowper was one of the last British painters to be influenced by the Pre-Raphaelites. Even in this late work their influence can be seen in the choice of medieval subject and late Romantic style. The scene is from Malory's* Morte d'Arthur: *four British queens find the Arthurian hero asleep beneath an apple tree. The sorceress Morgan le Fay attempts to make him take one as a lover, but he remains faithful to Guinevere. Cowper contemporizes the subject by portraying the queens as 1950s starlets admiring a film star.*

Culhwch and Olwen

The following tale of Culhwch and Olwen is one of the best known stories from the Mabinogion collection and one of the earliest tales in which King Arthur appears. References to iron and blacksmiths suggest a Celtic Iron-Age setting for the story; in which case it takes place in the cultural period of the 'genuine' Arthur. The hunt for a fabulous boar is a feature of the heroic myths of many cultures, as is the setting of impossible tasks by a tyrannical king in order to win a bride. Typical Celtic themes include the jealous stepmother, age-old talking animals and the freeing of a prisoner, subjects equally popular in folk–tales. Also of a particularly Celtic nature are the colourful descriptions of the attributes of Culhwch and Olwen.

The story is rich in British mythical characters, the most significant of whom is Mabon, the Celtic God of Youth. Culhwch's quest to free the ancient god might suggest that the original myth reflected a serious religious ritual, which involved the symbolic rediscovery of a lost god. However, by the medieval period such original mythical meanings would have become lost beneath the breathtaking excitement of the surface narrative.

Culhwch's birth was followed by the death of his mother. But before she died she made the king, her husband Celyddon Wledig, swear that he would not take another wife until a wild rose-bush with a pair of blossoms appeared on her grave. Several years later the flowering bush appeared and Celyddon married King Doged's widow. She immediately told her stepson, Culhwch, that he would marry no other woman than Olwen of the court of Arthur.

Culhwch therefore rode to the court of King Arthur, who was a cousin. How impressed were Arthur and his nobles when the youth rode into their courtyard! His horse was a beautiful grey, covered with a square purple cloth, a golden apple embroidered on each corner; the bridle and saddle, stirrups and shoes were of gold. The horse's hooves cast up the soil as it cantered, as though four swallows were ever around the youth's head. In each hand Culhwch held a silver spear, at his thigh was a sword of gold, its blade inlaid with a cross the colour of lightning, and alongside him trotted a pair of brindled greyhounds, their breasts gleaming white, with ruby-studded collars. The onlookers were amazed to see the blades of grass untouched by their passage, so light of foot was the horse.

Arthur welcomed the handsome stranger and offered him a high seat at the evening banquet. 'Sir, I come not for food and drink,' said Culhwch, 'but to ask a favour from you.'

'You will receive anything on earth or from sea which lies under wind, rain and sun,' replied Arthur, 'except for my ships, sword, shield, cloak and spear, or the hand of my Queen Guinevere.'

'Then I ask for Olwen, daughter of Yspaddaden,' said Culhwch.

'I have never heard of this woman,' said Arthur, 'but my men will search for her for one year, until when you will stay as my guest.'

A year later the men returned with nothing. 'You have failed to grant me my sole request,' said Culhwch, 'and I shall leave this place with a part of your honour.'

'How dare you insult our king?' cried Cei (Kay). 'Come with us and see for yourself that the woman is nowhere to be found.' Cei was one of the wonderful heroes of Arthur's court. He could hold his breath for nine days and nights under water; a wound from his sword could never be healed; and he could grow in an instant to the height of a tree.

Arthur selected Cei and several other heroes to accompany Culhwch on his quest. With them went Bedwyr (Bedivere) the One-Handed: no other man in the kingdom save Arthur himself could outrun him, his spear had the power of nine spears, and his single hand had the strength of three warriors on the battlefield. Kynthelig, the guide, went with them also; and Gwalchmai (Gawain), nephew and heir to Arthur, who had never returned from a quest unfulfilled; and Menw who could cast a magic spell over the party to make them disappear in hostile places. Gwrhyr went also, for he could speak the language of men and animals.

The heroes rode through the mountains for many days until they came to a great open plain. In the far distance they saw a magnificent castle, but although they rode straight towards it, several days passed before it began to loom above them. Outside the castle they found a giant shepherd with flocks of sheep which stretched to the horizon. They told the herdsman, whose name was Custennin, of their quest, but the giant warned them off, saying that no man had ever left the castle alive. They offered him a gold ring in return for information about Olwen, and he sent them to his wife who dwelt in a cottage beside the castle. The woman came running out to greet them, and went to embrace Cei, who quickly picked up a log from the woodpile and thrust it between the woman's arms to take his place; afterwards, the log fell to the ground, twisted and broken.

RIGHT **Kilhwych, the King's Son** (*tempera on wood by Arthur Joseph Gaskin, 1862–1928). Gaskin's interest in the early Italian painters is evident in his use of tempera paint as well as in the curious perspective and flat forms seen here. This style was intentionally medieval, as was his choice of Arthurian subjects: Culhwch appears as a courtly huntsman from the Age of Chivalry. The great contrast between the finely attired prince and the homespun clothes of the whipper-in may reflect Gaskin's Socialist leanings.*

'What an affectionate greeting!' said Cei. 'If that log had been me, no one would ever have hugged me again.'

They entered the cottage and the strange woman gave them dinner. Afterwards they asked her about Olwen. 'The girl comes here every seven days to bathe and wash her clothes,' said the old woman, 'but you must swear not to do her any harm, for she is the fairest maiden in the kingdom.' And Olwen walked in. She wore a silken robe the colour of flaming fire with a collar of reddish gold, set with rubies and emeralds. Her hair was more golden than yellow broom flowers, and her skin was whiter than foam on the wave-crest. The fingers on her hands were fairer than the wood anemones that grow beside the spring. Her eyes glanced and gleamed like those of the falcon. Like the downy breast of the swan were her breasts, her cheeks were like red roses, and all who saw her felt great love for her. White three-leaved flowers sprang up in her footsteps, which led to her being named Olwen, meaning 'White Track'.

Culhwch told her of his love for her since he had heard her lovely name in childhood, and Olwen returned his love but told him that he must perform the tasks set by her father Yspaddaden, if he was to win her hand. Thereupon Olwen took Culhwch and his companies up to the castle and introduced them to Yspaddaden Pencawr, her royal father. 'Lift up the skin which has fallen over my eyes,' said Yspaddaden, 'so that I might see what kind of man desires to be my son-in-law.'

When Yspaddaden had seen Culhwch, he sent the group away after they had been promised an answer by the next morning; but as they walked off, the old king threw a poisoned dart at their backs. Bedwyr heard it whistling through the air, caught it, and hurled it back at Yspaddaden, catching him on the knee. 'Is that the way for a son-in-law to treat me?' cried the king. 'I shall have an eternal limp because of his discourtesy.'

The warriors returned to the cottage of Custennin the Giant, and the next day visited Yspaddaden for his decision. 'I must ask the permission of the four great-grandparents of Olwen,' said the king, but as they walked away he threw a second dart at them; this time it was Menw who returned the iron dart to its owner, piercing his breast. 'A curse on such an ungentlemanly son-in-law,' cried Yspaddaden. 'I shall never climb the hill again without a pain in my chest.'

On the following day the warriors once more sought an audience with Yspaddaden, and again he threw a dart at their backs. Culhwch caught it in the air and in a second the dart was through the eye of Yspaddaden and out the back of his head. 'I shall never see the same again,' said the king, 'due to the insolence of a son-in-law. A curse on the smith who forged the iron darts.' They sat down together to eat, and Yspaddaden turned to Cylhwch and said: 'So it is you who wishes for the hand of my daughter. Firstly you must swear never to unjustly harm me. Secondly you must bring to me whatever I ask of you. Only then shall my daughter be yours.'

'Make your request,' answered Culhwch.

'My hair and beard have not been cut for years,' said Yspaddaden, 'and the only comb, razor and scissors which will do the job are between the ears of the monstrous boar, Twrch Trwyth. Fetch me those implements and my daughter is yours. One word of advice I give you: enlist the help of Mabon the Hunter. Only he can hunt the boar with his dog Drudwyn; but no one has seen him since he was stolen from his mother when only three days old. You must find his kinsman Eidoel, who might be able to tell you where Mabon now dwells.'

Culhwch and the warriors of Arthur set out on the next stage of his quest. They soon found Eidoel who took them to seek the advice of an

The warriors returned to Arthur, who assembled his whole army to besiege the castle at Gloucester. During the battle Cei and Gwrhyr entered the dungeon from the river and rescued Mabon on the back of the salmon, and thereupon, Arthur called upon all the warriors of the islands of Britain to accompany them on the hunt for the boar, Twrch Trwyth. At that time it was living in Ireland with seven young pigs. The dogs were loosed upon the boar and they chased him until they reached the sea, a fifth of Ireland lain to waste behind them. Twrch Trwyth swam the sea to Wales, and Arthur and his companions followed boar and hounds to dry land. As the hunt progressed through Wales, one by one the seven pigs were killed, although the boar also killed many of Arthur's champions.

They came at last to the River Severn and the boar was about to swim across it to Cornwall when Mabon, son of Modron appeared. He rode at the boar and skilfully snatched the razor from between its ears. Cei likewise took the scissors, but the beast turned into the river estuary with the comb still safely lodged in the hair of its neck. It was on the shores of Cornwall that the comb was finally taken after a great struggle, and Twrch Trwyth disappeared into the deep sea, never to be seen again.

The warriors returned to the castle of Yspaddaden and cursed the king for the deaths he had caused. The king's beard was shaved right down to the bone.

'Is that a close enough shave?' asked Culhwch.

'It is,' said Yspaddaden, 'and my daughter is yours. But you would never have won her without help from Arthur for I would not have given her up of my own free will; and so I die as I lose her.'

In this way did Culhwch meet and take to wife Olwen, the daughter of Yspaddaden Pencawr.

RIGHT
'Maponus' head from Corbridge, Northumberland, England (c. second to fourth centuries AD). The stone head has a hollow carved in its crown for libations. Maponus was the divine Youth of northern Britain.

RIGHT **Pagan Celtic stone figures** (Boa Island, Lough Erne, County Fermanagh, Ireland; c. fifth to seventh centuries AD). The double-sided figures stand in a Christian graveyard but retain the stylized, staring features of pagan Celtic images.

RIGHT **Reconstructed portal to a Celtic shrine** (Roquepertuse, Bouches-du-Rhône, France; third to second centuries BC). Niches in the columns contained the human skulls of fit young men, probably head-hunted in battle; a stone bird stood on the cross-beam.

Celtic Religion

Our understanding of Celtic religion is hindered, perhaps more than any other aspect of the Celtic world, by the lack of written sources and the difficulties involved in interpreting archeological evidence. These problems are increased by the secret nature of many Celtic religious cults, which was in part due to the great political respect commanded by Celtic priests and their consequent elitism.

Therefore we have to turn to the limited observations of ancient non-Celtic authors, whose writings are biased by their view of the Celts as primitive barbarians. The Greek Diodorus of Sicily, writing his 'mythical history' in the first century BC, refers (Book V, 31) to the high social status and learning of the Celtic Druids: 'Those men called by us philosophers and theologians are held in great honour by them; they call them "Druids" . . . and no sacrifice may be performed without a Druid present . . . for only they speak the language of the gods.' This Druidic control of religious affairs accounts for the many occasions in myth when they are consulted by clan-chiefs and kings – like ancient Greek oracles, they were able to influence political decisions. Julius Caesar tells us in his *Gallic War* (Book VI, 13–18) that the Druidic system originated in Britain and was exported to Gaul. He too refers to their great authority in Celtic society not only in religion, but also in educational and legal affairs, adding that their privileges included exemption from military service and taxation. Students of Druidic religion had to 'learn many verses by heart, sometimes for a period of 20 years. It is considered sacrilege to put their teachings into writing.' Celtic religion was thus *intended* to be mysterious and exclusive.

The importance of prophets in Celtic religion was also recorded by Diodorus: 'These men predict the future by observing the flight and calls of birds, and by the sacrifice of holy animals: all orders of society are in their power . . . and in very important matters they prepare a human victim, plunging a dagger into his chest; by observing the way his limbs convulse as he falls and the gushing of his blood, they are able to read the future.' Recent archeology has provided evidence to support such statements made by Greek and Roman writers that the Celts practised human sacrifice. Excavations in the 1980s of a sacred Gallic site at Ribemont in Picardy, France, revealed pits filled with human bones, the thigh bones purposefully arranged into right-angled patterns. This sanctuary was levelled by Julius Caesar during his conquest of Gaul. The body of 'Lindow Man', recently discovered in a Cheshire peat bog (now in the British Museum in London), might also have been the victim of Druidic sacrifice.

The names of Celtic deities are known from references in later myths and from religious inscriptions of the Roman period in Gaul and Britain. However, there are several reasons why their natures and mythical 'biographies' remain elusive compared to the many surviving divine stories of other ancient cultures. Celtic artists rarely produced anthropomorphic (human) images before they came under Greek influence during the 'La Tène' period (between the third and the first centuries BC). Therefore the relatively late artistic representations of Celtic divinities, produced by artists trained in the Graeco-Roman style, are not very helpful in telling us about original Celtic perceptions of their gods. Likewise it is difficult to unravel information about pagan religious ritual from Celtic literature as Christian writers would later have adapted or omitted any blatant pagan elements. However, some scholars have argued that the underlying structures of many of the myths reflect their original significance in Druidic religious rituals, with the texts containing many significant pagan details.

Celtic divinities as well as religious rituals became intermingled with their Graeco-Roman counterparts during the period of Roman domination. Mercury, a god of merchants and 'inventor of all the arts', found his Celtic equivalent in Lugh, who in Irish mythology is called 'skilled in all the arts'. Animal gods were important in Celtic religion, and Epona, particularly revered as a horse goddess, was even worshipped by the Romano-British cavalry. Cernunnos ('the horned one') is connected not only with the stag, but with bulls, rams and other powerful male animals. Both hunter and protector of animals, Cernunnos has persisted in British folk traditions as Herne the Hunter.

Celtic goddesses and gods represented the elemental forces of nature, and according to classical writers, their shrines tended to be in secluded groves. Many of these sacred sites must have disappeared, and our knowledge of ritual activities is mainly limited to the monumentalized religious sanctuaries of the Roman period. Although

ABOVE **St Bride** (John Duncan; tempera on canvas, 1913). The pagan Celtic goddess Brigit was daughter of Dagda, one of the original Irish gods, the Tuatha de Danaan. Around AD 450 she was transformed into the Christian St Brigit, founder of the first nunnery at Kildare. A Scottish legend tells of her travelling from Iona to Bethlehem and returning with the baby Jesus. Duncan portrays her equally as the pagan bringer of Spring, being carried by angels across the Sound of Iona.

absolute evidence is lacking, Druidic religious rituals probably also took place at pre-Celtic monuments such as stone circles. The Celtic religious year revolved around the control of the seasons and nature by sun and moon, and topographical 'focuses' of worship were ordained. Thus the Irish Druids met at Visnech, the 'navel' of Ireland, and Stonehenge in the south of England may also have been such a centre.

The Celtic year was divided into summer and winter. Summer began on the first of May, after the feast of Beltain on May-Eve. During this festival in honour of 'the fire of Bel' (Irish Bile was an ancient god of life and death), domestic fires were extinguished and rekindled from a new Druidic fire. Winter began on the first of November, preceded by the feast of Samhain (our Hallowe'en) when, in Ireland, the Sidhe (fairies of the Otherworld) were believed to be abroad signalling the time of the dead.

EIGHT

Tristan and Isolt

The story of Tristan and Isolt has undergone many transformations since it first appeared in pagan Celtic times. Hundreds of different versions have been written since the medieval period, culminating in one of the greatest expressions of nineteenth century Romanticism, Wagner's opera Tristan and Isolde. Modern scholars have traced these later accounts back to two main medieval literary strands: the twelfth-century poetry of the Anglo-Norman Thomas d'Angleterre and the German Eilhart von Oberg, and the prose romances of thirteenth-century France. Two other twelfth-century versions, by the French poet Beroul (arguably the earliest surviving written account) and a short anonymous episode, Tristan's Madness, were not used by later authors. Each of these five early accounts probably derived from one original written version, no longer extant. This hypothetical first written version must have been the culmination of an oral tradition dating back to the pre-Christian Celtic storytellers.

The arguments for Celtic origin lie mainly in the topography of the story, which takes us through most of the early Celtic areas, although the episodes in later Celtic Brittany also suggest a post-Christian adaptation. The medieval accounts placed King Mark of Cornwall's castle at Tintagel, with its Arthurian connotations: by the thirteenth century the story had become part of mainstream Arthurian legend. Tristan's native country was Lyonesse in the early versions: tradition places this lost land off the coast of Cornwall, and there are many local Cornish legends of forests and tolling bells beneath the sea. Lyonesse might also have been a mythical name (it derives from the Celtic sun-deity Lugh) for the Pictish area of Lothian. Medieval literary patrons such as Eleanor of Aquitaine

RIGHT **Tintagel Castle, Cornwall, England.** *Remains of the thirteenth-century castle can be seen overlooking the high cliffs (centre right). The modern bridge from mainland to island is also visible (bottom left).*

encouraged their 'troubadours' to produce new versions of the old love stories which would both emphasize the contemporary ideology of 'courtly love', as well as bring them into line with current religious attitudes. The trend for 'medieval revivals' seen in nineteenth-century Europe inspired Romantic interpretations of the rediscovered poems. Wagner's main source was the German poem of Gottfried von Strassburg (c. 1210), but the story had personal relevance to Wagner in reflecting his own love affair with his best friend's wife, Mathilde Wesendonck. Tennyson and other Victorian poets also produced versions of the story.

The underlying pagan Celtic nature of the story has never been lost: it is difficult to entirely Christianize or tame a story which deals with an adulterous love affair. Many even believe that the love potion was a post-Christian addition which provided an excuse for the lovers' sinful behaviour. However, it would seem likely that this is a Christian interpretation of an original Celtic feature as magical devices are common in Celtic mythology and reflect Druidic religious ritual. Ironically, the monks of Lindisfarne Priory still make a love potion from a secret recipe! The upbringing and heroic adventures of Tristan recall the deeds of the Irish CuChulainn and the Welsh Pryderi. Likewise, the strong and uncompromising characterization of Isolt and indeed the basic plot itself are paralleled in the stories of Irish Deirdre and Welsh Branwen. There is no 'authentic' version of Tristan and Isolt: major details of the plot differ from one account to another and the driving motives of the main characters vary according to the intentions of poet and audience. Some of the better known episodes are here incorporated into a prose version, omitting the blatantly Christian and medieval elements. However, some medieval French troubadour lays are included to enhance the narrative in the Celtic manner.

King Mark was ruler of Cornwall and dwelt in a fort at Tintagel, an impregnable stronghold on a high rocky promontory overlooking the Irish Sea. Cornwall was at war with Ireland and Mark's ally, Rivalin of Lothian, sailed down from Scotland to join in the struggle. As a sign of gratitude, Mark allowed Rivalin to return to Lothian with his sister as a wife. She died while giving birth to a son who, born in the midst of sorrow, was named Tristan.

Tristan was educated by Gorvenal, a wise and trusted member of Rivalin's court; the boy learnt all the arts of fighting and diplomacy, hunting and swimming. One day, when Tristan was sitting on the cliffs playing his harp to the sea birds, Gorvenal saw that the boy was ready: 'Young Tristan,' he said, 'I have taught you everything I know, and it is time for you to see what lies beyond the bounds of Lothian.'

'But where shall I go?' asked Tristan.

'To where the winds blow you and to where your heart guides you.'

And Tristan, with his tutor Gorvenal as companion, sailed to the land of his mother in Cornwall. As they approached Tintagel Fort, Tristan turned to his men: 'None of you', he said, 'are to tell these noble people who I am. For if I am to be received by them, it must be out of respect for my behaviour and not my royal title.'

King Mark welcomed them honourably into his fort, and that evening invited them to the banquet. Once the wine was flowing he turned to his guests: 'Strangers,' he said, 'tell us who you are and from where you have come.'

ABOVE **Ornamented 'Q', the first letter of the Latin version of St Luke's Gospel** *(illuminated manuscript of the Gospels, Lindisfarne, Northumbria, England; c. 698 AD). Christian monks working in Celtic areas often ornamented their Christian manuscripts in a Celtic style; pagan monsters and human figures often appear among the interwoven patterns. The use of expensive colours such as gold and silver meant that the material value of these spiritual texts increased the likelihood of Viking raids on the monasteries.*

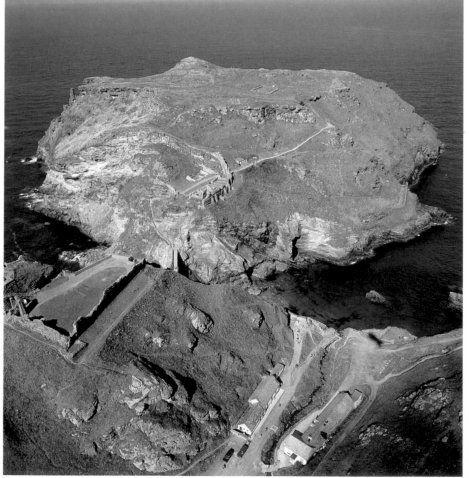

LEFT **Aerial view of Tintagel, Cornwall, England.** *The Lower Ward of the thirteenth-century castle is visible on the mainland (centre left). A modern bridge leads to a steep cliff-path which climbs up to the castle's Island Ward. On the summit of the Island are remains of the medieval Christian chapel. Archeologists have found evidence of an earlier, wealthy post-Roman stronghold on the Island contemporary with the 'Arthurian' Age, c. 450–600 AD). Local medieval legends associated the site with the birth of Arthur, while others saw it as King Mark's castle and the setting for tales of Tristan and Isolt.*

'We come from the north,' answered Tristan, 'and our fathers are merchants; but none of us has a heart for trading, and so we offer ourselves as warriors in your service.' Tristan then made music and the whole room fell quiet at the plaintive melodies of his harp.

'You shall stay here gladly,' said King Mark.

For over a year Tristan and his men from Lothian remained at Tintagel. The war with Ireland had ended with a treaty in which Mark had promised to send annual tribute to the King of Ireland. With the arrival of the warriors of Lothian Mark decided to refuse the payments, which consisted of the enslavement of young Cornish boys and girls, and thus came the chance that Tristan was waiting for to prove himself to the king.

FAR RIGHT **Door column of the Church of St Mary and St David, Kilpeck, near Hereford, England** *(twelfth century* AD*). Late Celtic warriors are interlaced with dragons in the pagan decorations of the Church exterior.*

RIGHT **Stone head** *(Salzburg, Austria; c. first century* BC *to first century* AD*). The Celts believed heads to contain magical properties: the heads of the enemy were greatly valued as battle-prizes and there are many mythical references to powerful heads. Carved stone heads probably had similar ritual significance.*

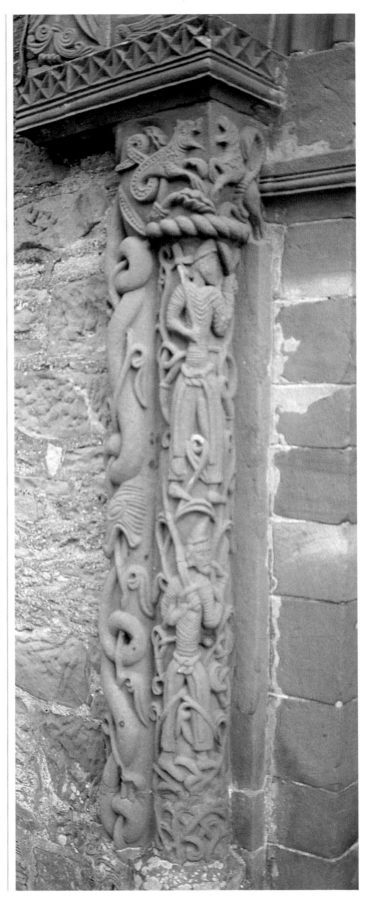

A new champion had emerged in Ireland; he was Morholt, brother of the Irish queen and a great warrior. Tristan was the first to see Morholt's ship sailing towards Tintagel and he knew what he was coming for. Morholt beached his ship and sent a message to the king demanding the tribute. 'He shall not have it', said Tristan, 'without a fight.' As there were no other volunteers to meet Morholt in single combat, Mark agreed to Tristan's request to do so with a promise that he would be raised to the nobility of Cornwall if he succeeded.

Morholt accepted the challenge but on condition that his adversary was of equal royal bearing to himself.

Tristan could no longer conceal his real identity from the court of Tintagel: 'I am the son of King Rivalin of Lothian,' he said, 'and nephew to King Mark of Cornwall.' King Mark was at once happy and sad that this fine young man was his sister's son, and yet he was to risk his life for Cornwall. Tristan, however, would not be dissuaded and it was agreed that the fight would take place on a small island opposite Tintagel.

At dawn on the appointed day, Tristan rowed out towards the island, and seeing Morholt's boat drawn up on the beach, he abandoned his own and waded ashore. Morholt was clearly puzzled by this behaviour: 'Why did you push your boat out to sea?' he asked.

'Only one of us will be leaving this island today,' answered Tristan, drawing his sword and striking the first blow.

The sea birds were the only witnesses to the long and bloody battle. The final blow was struck by Tristan: his sword smashed through Morholt's helmet, splitting his skull. Morholt was taken from the island in the Irish ship, while Tristan rowed the small boat back to Tintagel where there was much rejoicing that night. But Tristan was strangely troubled: his sword had splintered and a small fragment was missing.

Morholt died on the sea voyage home and there was great mourning in Ireland for the death of their hero.

The king's daughter, whose name was Isolt, had been taught the magic properties of herbs by her mother. While attempting to revive Morholt with her craft, she extracted a piece of sharp metal from his fractured head. She wrapped it in silk knowing that one day she would discover the sword from which it came: on that day she would avenge her uncle.

Tristan had suffered a small wound from Morholt's spear, but did not realise at first that it had been dipped in one of the poisons brewed by Isolt of Ireland. The wound began to fester and soon no one would approach Tristan's room for the stench. Tristan knew that the antidote for the poison lay somewhere across the sea and he had himself pushed out into the ocean where he drifted for many days. Manannan the Sea God watched over him and blew his boat gently towards Ireland. When the land came into view Tristan took up his harp and sang. The people of Dublin were amazed at the sight of the boat without a pilot. As it drew nearer they heard the soft sounds of a sweet harp playing and a voice singing. The music enchanted them and they drew the boat ashore and carried the wounded minstrel, who called himself Tantris, to the court. There he was tended by the maids of Princess Isolt and cured by her herbs: but the two never met before it came time for Tristan to return to Cornwall.

LEFT **Iron-Age settlement, Chysauster, Cornwall, England** (c. *first century* BC *to third century* AD). *The well-preserved remains of nine 'courtyard houses' at Chysauster reveal a stone-paved passage leading into an open courtyard, off which open several small rooms. Originally with thatched roofs, the houses had drains and terraced gardens.*

ABOVE **Warrior fights monster** *(bronze matrix for making decorative helmet plaques, from Torslunda, Sweden; eighth century* AD). *The* Teutonic warriors of pre-Viking Sweden, like their Celtic neighbours, decorated their helmets with scenes of power. Here, a warrior with axe confronts a wild beast.

In Cornwall, he had long been given up for dead and great was the rejoicing at his homecoming; but there were some in Mark's court who were jealous of the affection which the foreigner Tristan had inspired in their king, and they planned to find Mark a wife, in the hope that a son would be born and inherit Cornwall. The king was aware of their schemes and one day found a reason for putting off the marriage for ever. It was early summer and Mark was sitting by a window looking out to sea. The swallows were swooping low over the cliffs and one of them dropped a ruddy golden thread into his lap. Mark ran it through his fingers and realized that it was a woman's hair. At the feast that evening Mark held up the long fair hair: 'Many of you,' he said, 'wish to see me married; but I shall marry no one except the owner of this hair. There will be great rewards for the man who discovers her and brings her back to Cornwall.'

'I killed Morholt for you,' said Tristan, 'and I shall find you a wife.'

Tristan set sail from Tintagel with his friends and Manannan blew up a great storm which shipwrecked them on the coast near Dublin. The men of Lothian disguised themselves as merchants and stood around in the markets listening out for clues to the owner of the golden hair; but the news was not of women but of dragons. The countryside around Dublin was being devastated by a fire-breathing monster and the King of Ireland had offered the hand of his daughter Isolt to the man who brought him evidence of the creature's death. Tristan instinctively set out to find the dragon, following the scorched earth towards its lair, where he sat and waited for the monster's return.

Tristan was gazing at the full moon when against it appeared the black shadow of the dragon. The air grew hot as it approached and Tristan caught sight of it in the moonlight as it flew towards the den. It was a white dragon with huge flapping wings and a long pointed tail; along its spine ran a line of poisonous thorns and its teeth gleamed razor-sharp. Tristan confronted the monster which roared and shot out billows of white smoke from its nostrils, enshrouding him in a mist. Tristan could see nothing until suddenly the clouds were broken by the dragon's opening jaws. Tristan's reactions were fast and he plunged his spear into its throat, performed the salmon leap onto its neck and reached over to slice off the dragon's poisonous forked tongue. He put the tongue inside his stocking and set off for Dublin; but the warmth of his body drew out the poison and Tristan collapsed on the path which led to the dragon's lair.

The Irish king's steward, who secretly lusted after Isolt, had been watching the whole battle from a tree; he hacked off the dragon's head and took it to the King, claiming his prize. Isolt shrank at the thought of marrying this man, who was considered a liar and coward by many in the court. Therefore she went with her mother and Brangaine, her maid-servant, to the dragon's lair; there they found Tristan unconscious, with the forked tongue in his hand, and they carried him between them back to the court. Brangaine then recognized him as Tantris, the minstrel they had tended months earlier, and Tristan continued to hide his true identity.

It was several weeks before Tristan began to recover with the help of Isolt's herbs. Isolt had become increasingly attracted to this stranger, who even on his sick-bed played the harp so beautifully. It seemed curious to her that such a minstrel should also be a valiant fighter, and she hoped in her heart of hearts that he would survive the dragon's poison and claim her as his prize.

The day came for him to leave his bed and while he was bathing Isolt cleaned his armour. The notch on his sword caught her notice and she ran to her room to find the silk-wrapped

LEFT **Gaullish prisoner** (c. *first century* BC). *This Roman bronze depicts the Celt as a stereotyped heroic enemy, hands tied behind back. Trousers were favoured by Celtic chieftains from the Hallstatt period onwards, whereas Irish aristocrats wore knee-length tunics and cloaks. Aristocratic Celtic women also wore tunics and cloaks.*

105

splinter which not so long ago she had removed from her uncle's head: the piece perfectly fitted the notch in the minstrel's sword. At that moment Isolt's feelings of love for Tristan turned to hatred. 'So at last the gods have brought you to me,' she said to him. 'You are the man who slew my uncle Morholt. On that mournful day when I realized that my herbs had no power over death, I swore that one day I would have my revenge.'

'I killed Morholt in single combat,' said Tristan, 'and on behalf of my king. There was no treachery in your uncle's death, but treachery will triumph if you kill me, for then you must marry the steward who lays claim to the dragon-slaying. I am the only man who can prove him false.' And Isolt stormed out of the room, and neither of them could sleep that night.

The next day the court gathered to hear the steward make his official claim to Isolt. 'It was no easy task,' he said holding up the dragon's head, 'but I suffered no wounds and will defend you equally well when the next monster arrives.'

'You are that lying monster,' cried Isolt, 'and here is the man who truly killed the dragon.' Tristan was led into the hall.

'Prove it!' spat the steward.

'This coward has the head,' said Tristan, 'but I have the deadly tongue. I am Tristan, royal nephew of the King of Cornwall. I was sent here to find the owner of this golden hair, and I think that in killing the dragon, I have found her.' And Tristan held up the dragon's tongue in one hand and the hair in the other. Every man and woman present gasped, for the tongue was hideous and the hair beautiful: and every head turned from the cowering steward to the Princess Isolt.

'Your king shall have Isolt as his queen,' said the Irish king, 'and let this marriage bind a peace between our two countries.' The day before they left for Cornwall, Isolt's mother gave a powerful love potion to Brangaine: 'You are to slip half of this into the King of Cornwall's wine, and half into my daughter's on their wedding night. It will surely bind them together in love.'

The ship sailed out of Dublin harbour and Isolt stood at the stern and watched the sun setting in reds and golds over her land as it slipped away from her. For two days the sea was whipped up by the storm chariots of Manannan the Sea God; by the third day the winds had died away and the ship was strangely becalmed. The sun beat down on Tristan and Isolt as they played a board game to pass away the time: Isolt still would not speak to Tristan. She called Brangaine to fetch them a refreshing herbal drink from her travelling-chest. They drank, as was the custom, from the same bowl; and as they drank the winds blew and the sail filled, the waves lashed and the salt spray was in their hair. Their hands touched as they passed the bowl from one to the other, at first shyly and then with the full passion that the draught inspired: for Brangaine had mistakenly served them with the love potion.

The ship arrived at Tintagel and King Mark was highly pleased with Isolt. But it was not Isolt that he slept with on their wedding night. Tristan realized that the King would discover that he was not the first to make love to Isolt: therefore he persuaded Brangaine to slip into the marriage bed the moment the lights were extinguished. Thus began the many deceits that were to lead eventually to the discovery of Tristan and Isolt's secret love, for the lovers could not keep away from one another, try as they might. Both Tristan and Isolt felt much guilt, for each of them felt great affection towards Mark, but the love potion's magic was intended to last for three years and it was too strong for them to resist.

Those that had always been jealous of Tristan now found a way of putting him out of favour. It was not difficult for them to arouse the king's suspicions for Tristan and Isolt were ever flirting across the table at ban-

quets. One man in particular, Andret, who had a secret desire for Isolt, hoped that one day the lovers would be discovered. The rumours grew and Mark expelled Tristan from the court. Even so, Tristan and Isolt could not be parted. There was a spring in the orchard outside the walls of Tintagel which flowed as a stream into the fort; Tristan would hide up a tree in the orchard and throw summer flowers or twigs in winter into the stream as a sign to Isolt that he was waiting for her. Andret asked a Druid to determine from the stars whether the two were still seeing one another. The Druid saw it all in the night sky: the orchard, the flowers in the stream and Isolt slipping out of the fort.

One day the Druid predicted that a lover's tryst was to take place while the king was out hunting the wild boar that night. Andret therefore schemed to bring the king back home earlier than expected at the following dawn. Tristan and Isolt met among the night-scented flowers of the orchard while Brangaine kept watch as usual from the tower above Isolt's chamber. As the first glimmers

of dawn were touching the starry sky
Brangaine sang:

> 'God of light which makes
>   things true and clear,
> Please be faithful and help my
>   companions,
> For I have not seen them
>   since twilight
> And before long will it be
>   dawn.
>
> 'Fine companions, whether
>   you sleep or are waking,
> Sleep no more, my masters, if
>   you please.
> For in the eastern sky the star
>   ascends
> Which heralds the day which
>   I knew would come,
> And before long will it be
>   dawn.
>
> 'Fine companions, my song is
>   calling you,
> Sleep no more, for I hear the
>   bird singing
> As it looks for the day
>   amongst the thickets.
> And I fear that the jealous
>   man is after you,
> And before long will it be
>   dawn.'

Tristan returned her song:

> 'Beautiful sweet companion,
>   so rich is this place,
> That I wish that it would
>   never be dawn or day.
> For the woman I hold in my
>   arms
> Is the most beautiful ever
>   born of a mother,
> And that is why I care so
>   little
> For the jealous fool and the
>   dawn . . .'

Tristan's song was interrupted by
King Mark and his warriors, who had
crept into the orchard guided by
Andret. The two lovers were bound
and immediately their punishment
was pronounced: Tristan and Isolt

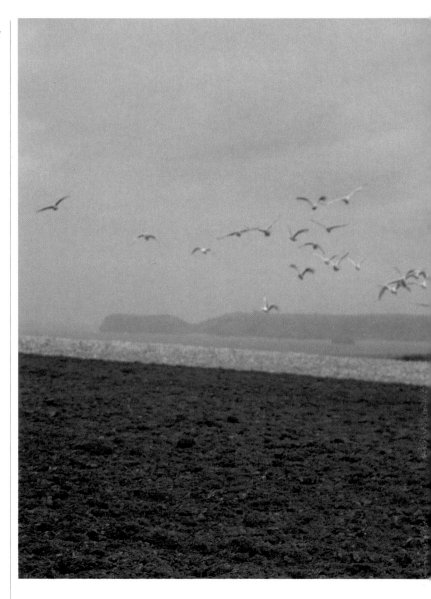

were to be burnt in a pit of flaming
branches. On their way to the place
of death, Tristan was allowed to make
an offering of appeasement to the
angry gods on a sacred rock above the
sea. 'Save yourself!' cried Isolt. 'If you
live then I shall also live in death.'
And Tristan leapt into the sea; so
high was the cliff that all who saw
him jump considered him dead. The
only sound was the crying of sea gulls.

'A fine sacrifice to Manannan the
Sea God,' said Mark, and Isolt was
taken to the death-pit. A group of
diseased men who lived in the woods
surrounding Tintagel approached the
place. 'Since Queen Isolt is to die
anyway,' said one of them, his face

ABOVE **Distant view
of the headland at
Tintagel, Cornwall,
England.** *The
legendary birthplace of
King Arthur was also
believed in local folklore
to have been the fortress
of King Mark. Tintagel
was its medieval name,
meaning 'The Fortress
of the Constriction' and
taken from the Celtic
words* din *(fort) and*
tag *(obstruct or
construct). An apt
description for the
dramatic manner in
which the Island meets
the mainland.*

hideously pock-marked, 'why not give her to us for our pleasure. She will soon be dead, and her death will appease the evil demons who bring disease to your lands.' And Isolt was unbound and taken away.

Tristan had survived his plunge into the sea and lay in ambush for the captors of Isolt as they took her away to the woods. He had no difficulty in saving her from them, and Tristan and Isolt lived as outlaws in the woods for many months. The effects of the love potion, which had been brewed to last for three years, were wearing off: they had shared a beautiful dream and were waking into a world of harsh reality. Their love for one another became real, but so did their strong sense of remorse for having wounded the heart of King Mark. Tristan decided that he must leave Cornwall for Brittany; and Isolt returned to Tintagel and swore an oath of loyalty to her husband. Soon Isolt saw from her tower a small boat sailing southwards along the coast; and she knew that she would never see Tristan alive again.

Tristan landed in Brittany with his companion Gorvenal, and they offered themselves as warriors to the local king, whose name was Hoel. Tristan, who no longer cared whether he lived or died, immediately proved his courage in battle against a neighbouring tribe. That evening at the victory banquet, King Hoel stood up and announced: 'Today I have seen a new hero who is quite reckless in battle; as a reward I offer him my daughter, Isolt of the White Hands, as a wife.' Tristan was now as reckless in his drinking as he was at fighting. He looked at Isolt of the White Hands who had blushed the colour of the foxglove on the moor, reminding him of another Isolt. That night they slept together, but Tristan could not bring himself to make love to a distant heart. His excuse was that he was suffering from an old wound.

Isolt of the White Hands tolerated her husband's lack of interest and even began to joke about it with her maidservants. One day she was out hunting with her brother Kaherdin; as they were jumping a fence the mud splashed up and spattered her thighs: 'Why!' she laughed, 'even the mud is more interested in me than my husband.' And that evening Kaherdin questioned Tristan and discovered the real reason for his coldness; Tristan swore Kaherdin to silence by promising that he would make every effort to forget his former love.

The following day brought a surprise attack on Hoel's fort and Tristan was badly wounded. Isolt of the White Hands did not have the potent herbal cures of Isolt the Fair (as the men of Brittany called the Cornish queen). Tristan, realizing that he was going to die unless Isolt herself came to him, gave a message to Gorvenal to take to Cornwall: 'Tell the men of Cornwall that I am dying of a poisoned wound, and that only Queen Isolt can cure me. Go in my boat and if you return with Isolt, hoist the white sail, but if she will not come, then let the sail be black.' Isolt of the White Hands overheard the message and at last knew where Tristan's absent heart lay.

Several days later Tristan had become very weak and was on the threshold of the Underworld; suddenly he heard the watchmen of King Hoel's fort shouting that a boat was in view. 'What colour is the sail?' he asked his Breton wife. Isolt of the White Hands felt the jealousy well up inside her: 'It is black, my lord,' she replied. Tristan's heart burst within him as Isolt the Fair and King Mark came running into his room. Isolt stood above her dead lover and, hearing the sounds of his harp in her memory, sang:

> 'The sun is shining, clear and
>   fair,
> And I can hear the sweet
>   song of birds;
> All around me they sing in
>   the thickets
> And their songs are new.

BELOW **Head of the Celtic god Coriosolites** (*bronze coin from Brittany; first century* BC). *The Celts borrowed the idea of coinage from the Greeks and Romans; local kings portrayed themselves on the coins, together with symbols of their trade and wealth on the reverse, such as ears of corn or horses. This Gallic coin depicts a local god, with fashionable Celtic warrior hairstyle: note the chain with a severed head attached hanging from his hair. Diodorus refers to the Celtic custom of taking heads as proof of valour in battle, and such heads were sometimes offered to warrior gods.*

RIGHT **Gold boat model** (*from Broighter, County Derry, Ireland; first century* BC). *This miniature boat, complete with benches, mast and oars, was part of a hoard of gold jewellery and may have been an offering to a water deity such as the Irish sea god, Manannan.*

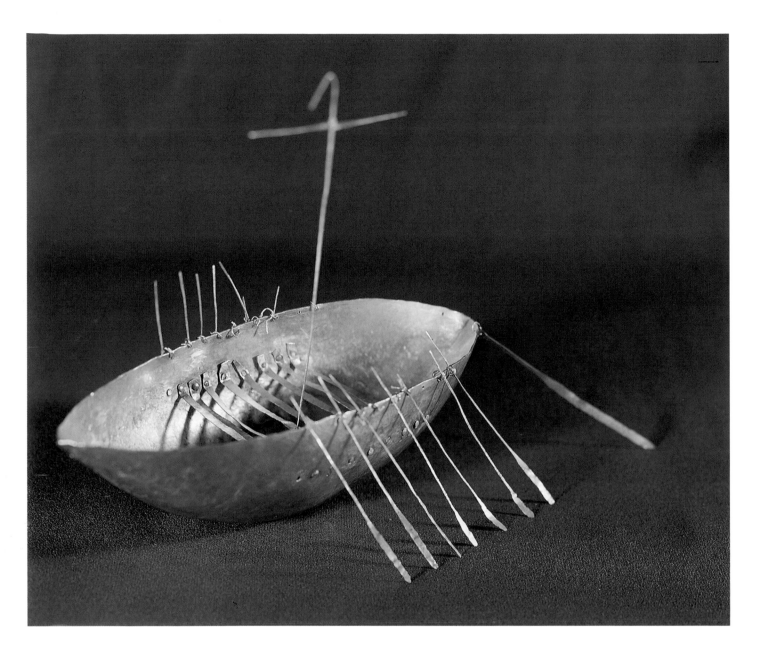

'I see my own death coming,
And I sing a lay which will be
    held most dear,
And will not fail to touch
    lovers,
For it is love which makes me
    long to die.

'Tristan, my friend, friend,
    friend,
Here is my heart which I
    entrusted
To your love; not a good
    place for it,
and now it will die by your
    sword.

'Tristan, my friend, friend,
    friend,
Even though the gods despise
    my desire,
My soul shall dwell in your
    spirit,
In the lands of the blessed or
    in the Underworld.'

Falling on Tristan's sword, Isolt
followed him to the Underworld, and
thus did the lovers return in death to
King Mark's fort at Tintagel. They
were buried in two mounds, side by
side, and the intertwining branches of
two trees grew from their graves.

THE ISLE OF MAN

The island's position in the Irish Sea between Ireland and Scotland has ensured it a place in Celtic mythology and tradition. It may have been considered one of the Isles of the Blessed, as was the island of Arran, ruled by the archaic Irish God of the Sea, Manannan (another child of Lir). The Manx language, closely related to Scottish Gaelic, was considered extinct by the 1950s, but there have been recent attempts at revival. An oral traditon of law, which might reflect original Druidic practice, had precedence, until recently, over written laws. Post-Celtic man was governed by Vikings until Scottish rule began in the thirteenth century. The following Manx folk–song has Christian references, but its themes of love vows, curses and powerful natural elements are those of Celtic mythology.

I first met my truelove at the Christmas ceilidh; we sat while the fiddler played and began our courting.

For seven whole years we met and made love, and her unfaithful tongue swore that she would never leave me.

On the Sunday before Ash Wednesday I visited by truelove; she placed her hands over mine and swore she would marry only me.

I came home in ecstasy, everything was roses; on the Wednesday I heard she had married another.

I cursed her for courting me for so long a time; when she found she had no love for me she should have said so.

But I cannot speak wickedly of her or call for bad luck; may she make her new friends glad, though love has a made a fool of me.

No one knew about our love save the old walnut tree; it cannot speak for me though it knows my lover false.

On St Patrick's Day I shall visit the fair in my young man's clothes, I'll walk right by her, pretending not to notice.

At the fair I'll take my pick from all the best girls; but she has no second chance with her deceitful new husband.

I walked the long winding road and grew weary of the slopes, but whenever I rested I thought of my love.

I wish that the wind would bring me news of my love; I wish she would cross the steep highlands to greet me and meet me by the shore.

How happily I would run to the shore if she were there; how happily my hand would make a pillow for her hair.

I wish that the sea would run dry and let me have my way; but the white snows of Greenland will sooner turn the red of roses before I forget my truelove.

LEFT **Madron Well, Cornwall, England.** *Sources of water were revered by the Celts for their religious powers, and many of these sacred springs and wells continued to be visited for spiritual healing in the Christian era, often dedicated to saints. Madron was also the site of a baptistry. Sick people still drink these waters and hang votive rags on the surrounding trees.*

BRITTANY

*I*n the fifth century, several noble Welsh families fled the Saxon invasion of their country and landed in France. The area later became known as 'Little Britain' or Brittany. The Bretons brought their Celtic language and mythology with them, but many of their stories have been lost owing to the French government's past ban on speaking Breton. Only folk-tales and songs have survived in the Breton tongue: the Breton singer and harpist, Alan Stivell, has led the recent revival. The following traditional ballad contains a reference to the Virgin Mary, but the common ancient Celtic theme of the sea as a setting for miraculous tales involving women is present in the song. It was collected from the singing of Janet ar Gall of Kerarborn in 1849.

It was the first of November when the English reached Dourduff.
They beached at Dourduff and snatched a young girl.
They snatched a lovely maiden and took her to their ship.
Her name was Marivonnik and she came from Plougasnou.
As they carried her away, she cried at her father's door:

'Fare thee well dear mother and father, for I'll never see you more.
'Fare thee well dear brother and sister, for we'll never meet on earth.
'Fare thee well kinsmen and friends, for I'll never see your world again.'
And young Marivonnik wept, with no one there to comfort her.
No one was there to comfort her save the big Englishman, he comforted her.
'Do not cry, my Marivonnik, your life is not at risk;
'Your life is not at risk, but I cannot save your honour.'
'Sir Englishman, my honour means more to me than all your ships at sea;
'Tell me then, shall I lose my honour to more than you alone?'
'To me and to my cabin boy, and to the sailors if they want you.
'To my sailors if they want you, every one hundred and one.'
'Tell me then, Sir Englishman, may I walk with you on the bridge?'
'You may walk up on the bridge, but take care not to drown.'
Young Marivonnik cried, whilst walking on the deck:
'Help me, Mary Virgin, shall I end it all by drowning?
'It is for you, dear Virgin Mary, so as not to offend you.
'If I fall in the sea, then drowned I shall be; if I stay I shall be killed.'
Young Marivonnik was guided by the Virgin and dived into the sea.
She was brought back to the surface by a small fish.
The big Englishman then called out to his sailormen:
'Sailors, sailors, rescue her and five hundred crowns are yours!'
And later that day he told young Marivonnik:
'You should not have done this, Marivonnik, for you were to be my wife.'

WALES

The Welsh language has survived in education and broadcasting, though what chance it stands against the English and American mass-media remains to be seen. The Mabinogion and Arthurian legends have survived in folk–tales as well as in high literature. The following story appears in the Journey Through Wales *by the twelfth–century churchman, Giraldus Cambrensis. In that Christianized version, Elidor is training to be a monk and runs away from his harsh teachers: I have omitted the Christian elements. The modern English author Alan Garner sets the story in Manchester where the escape is from urban squalor. The theme of the visit to the fairy world is one of the commonest in Celtic mythology. Such myths also provided the Celts with an 'explanation' for the great tomb mounds of the earlier Bronze–Age culture. The 'yellow ball' in this story is a fairy flower in other versions, all of which contain the feature of the fairy rule that you may not take anything back with you to the mortal world.*

E lidor was a young boy who was fed up with life. One day on the way to school he turned around and made his way to the woods. He wandered along the river in a dream and soon found himself at the entrance to a cave. Two little people came running out and said: 'Why don't you come inside and have some fun? Our world is happier than yours!'

Elidor did not stop to think, but followed them into the cave and found himself in a dark passageway which became narrower and lower until he was squeezing through on all fours. Just as he was beginning to panic the tunnel opened out into another cavern; they made for the light at the entrance and Elidor emerged into a world which he had only ever seen in paintings and dreams. It was an idyllic landscape with flowery meadows running down to lazy rivers; and yet there was something wrong too — Elidor looked up and saw that, although the world was bright, there was a mist hanging over everything so that neither sun, moon nor stars would shine.

Elidor was led before the king who asked who he was and from where he had come. The king was rather confused by the boy's answers and waved

RIGHT **Snowdonia.** *The highland region of north-west Wales has proved a difficult obstacle for Roman and English invaders. Many Welsh myths are located in the region, which provides a dramatic backdrop of lakes, streams and mountains.*

him away saying, 'You will remain here as a playmate for my son.' That afternoon, if indeed it was afternoon, Elidor stood back and watched the little people as they played. They were finely proportioned and most had long fair hair. Their riding was on horses the size of greyhounds, but they did not hunt for they did not eat meat, preferring milk flavoured with saffron. In their conversations they ridiculed Elidor's people for their lives of violence and deceit, yet they did not have any religious beliefs.

Elidor grew homesick and the king allowed him a visit to his mother on condition that he returned. The little people led him back into the cavern, through the cramped tunnel which became wider and higher, until they reached the cave by the river. Here Elidor left his tiny companions and returned to his mother's house. She asked him where he had been and begged him not to leave home again, but he told her of his promise to the king. Thus Elidor spent his time divided between the ordinary world and the land of the little people.

One day Elidor told his mother of the brilliant yellow balls that they played with in the other place. His mother asked him to bring one home for she was poor and thought that they must be golden. So the next time Elidor was playing with the little people he took one of the balls and ran off with it into the cavern, through the widening passage and back to his mother. But just as he entered the house a tiny foot tripped him up and he dropped his treasure. He turned just in time to see the two little people scowl at him and run off with the ball.

The following day Elidor went into the woods and walked along the river to the cave, but he could no longer find it. Many years later he would walk along the river with his own children and tell them again and again the story of the little people.

LEFT **A Spirit or Sidhe in a Landscape** (*oil on board by George William Russell, 1867–1935*). *The Irish artist's play* Deirdre *was performed in Dublin in 1902, and he is best known as a poet of works based on Celtic mythology. As a painter he tended to concentrate on a particular theme during a particular period. Between 1900–1905 he produced a series of images of Celtic spirits in landscape settings.*

SCOTLAND

RIGHT **Horseman
drinking** (Pictish stone
from Invergowrie, near
Dundee, Scotland; c.
ninth century AD). The
native Celtic Picts were
probably a continuation
of the Caledonian tribes
who resisted the Roman
invasion. Together with
the intrusive Irish
Scotti, they invaded the
Roman territory of
northern Britain in the
fourth and fifth
centuries AD. The
Pictish Kingdom
controlled northern
Britain between the
sixth and ninth
centuries, and
eventually joined with
the Scotti in the
formation of Scotland.
Horses were status
symbols in all Celtic
societies; here, the rider
drinks from a horn
which, with its eagle-
headed terminal, is a
further symbol of
power.

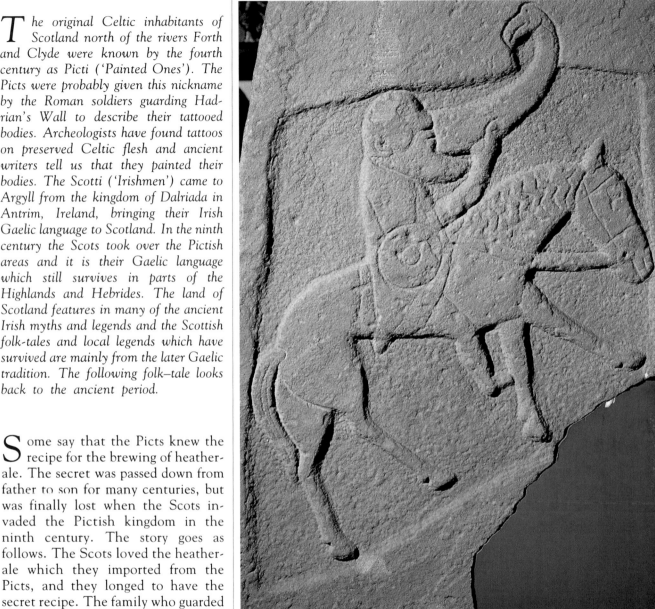

*T*he original Celtic inhabitants of Scotland north of the rivers Forth and Clyde were known by the fourth century as Picti ('Painted Ones'). The Picts were probably given this nickname by the Roman soldiers guarding Hadrian's Wall to describe their tattooed bodies. Archeologists have found tattoos on preserved Celtic flesh and ancient writers tell us that they painted their bodies. The Scotti ('Irishmen') came to Argyll from the kingdom of Dalriada in Antrim, Ireland, bringing their Irish Gaelic language to Scotland. In the ninth century the Scots took over the Pictish areas and it is their Gaelic language which still survives in parts of the Highlands and Hebrides. The land of Scotland features in many of the ancient Irish myths and legends and the Scottish folk-tales and local legends which have survived are mainly from the later Gaelic tradition. The following folk–tale looks back to the ancient period.

*S*ome say that the Picts knew the recipe for the brewing of heather-ale. The secret was passed down from father to son for many centuries, but was finally lost when the Scots invaded the Pictish kingdom in the ninth century. The story goes as follows. The Scots loved the heather-ale which they imported from the Picts, and they longed to have the secret recipe. The family who guarded the recipe lived in the Mull of Galloway in the far west of the Pictish kingdom. One day father and son were captured in battle and the Scots had them brought out onto the open moor high up above the sea where the purple heather used for the famous brew was growing all around them. The Scots demanded the recipe, threatening and torturing the old man and his young son until they were on the point of death.

RIGHT **Christy Moore.**
*The Irish singer/
songwriter continues the
tradition of the Celtic
bards by heroizing the
modern freedom-fighters
of Ireland and Central
America. He has sung
with the Irish folk group
Planxty as well as with
Moving Hearts, one of
the earliest bands to
combine folk, rock and
jazz styles. Here he is
playing the Irish
bodhran, a hand-held
drum.*

The sea-gulls were mewing as dusk began to fall. 'I shall tell you what you want to know,' spoke the old man at last, 'but only on condition that you first kill my son, so that he does not have the pain of witnessing his father bring dishonour and shame to our people.' The weary Scots raised a cry of victory and the boy was put to the sword. 'Now, old man,' they said, 'tell us the recipe.'

'Ha!' said the father, 'do you really think I would tell a Scot the secret of heather-ale? My son was about to divulge the recipe, for he still had many years to live and would not readily give up this beautiful world of sea-birds, high cliffs and the sounds of the foaming sea. Therefore he had to die; and the secret of heather-ale dies with him, for you will never have it from me!'

The Scottish chieftain was furious. 'Take him,' he cried, 'and hurl him from the highest cliff. Let him be smashed to pieces on the sharp rocks below, and may the sea mourn him forever more with her salty tears.'

Thus the old man died, and now shares the secret of heather-ale with the sea.

IRELAND

*F*or historical reasons the Celtic tradition has survived better in Ireland than in any of the other Celtic areas. Modern Irish Gaelic is a close descendant of the ancient Celtic language; it is still spoken in the southwest and was recognized as an official language by the Republic of Ireland in 1921. Many Celtic myths and legends have come down to us in Irish, and the Irish folk-tale tradition is equally strong. The following traditional ballad was first sung at the time of the mass emigrations to America by young Irish men and women seeking work after the Great Famine of the 1840s. This relatively

modern song is addressed to the legendary heroes of Ireland, a typical use of myth to conjure up a distant Golden Age. The emigrations themselves have now become legendary and the mythical power of the song remains relevant in a country still affected by emigration; it was recently recorded in 1983 by the Irish band Planxty.

You brave Irish heroes
wherever you be,
I pray stand a moment and
listen to me,
Your sons and fair daughters
are now going away,
And thousands are sailing to
Americay.

So good luck to those people
and safe may they land,
They are leaving their
country for a far distant
strand,
They are leaving old Ireland,
no longer can stay,
And thousands are sailing to
Americay.

The night before leaving they
are bidding goodbye,
And it's early next morning
their heart gives a sigh,
They do kiss their mothers
and then they will say
'Farewell, dear old father, we
must now go away.'

Their friends and relations
and neighbours also,
When the trunks are all
packed up, all ready to go,
O the tears from their eyes
they fall down like the
rain,
And the horses are prancing,
going off for the train.

So good luck to those people
and safe may they land,
They are leaving their
country for a far distant
strand,
They are leaving old Ireland,
no longer can stay,
And thousands are sailing to
Americay.

When they reach the station,
you will hear their last cry,
With handkerchiefs waving
and bidding goodbye,
Their hearts will be breaking
on leaving the shore,
'Farewell, dear old Ireland,
will we ne'er see you
more?'

O I pity the mother that rears
up the child,
And likewise the father who
labours and toils,
To try to support them he
will work night and day,
And when they are older they
will go away.

So good luck to those people
and safe may they land,
They are leaving their
country for a far distant
strand,
They are leaving old Ireland,
no longer can stay,
And thousands are sailing to
Americay.

ENGLAND

*I*n spite of the various invasions of *England from the Roman times onwards, there are still folk memories of the Celtic past when the Brythonic language was spoken. England has a good number of pagan Celtic folk-customs, from the corn dolly to Morris Dancing. Un-Christianized Arthurian legends have persisted in local folklore and many English folk–songs appear to stem back to a pagan Celtic origin.*

The 'high' subject matter of the following ballad suggests that it was composed for the court, but the colloquial language points to its later transformation into folk-song. The court bards were travellers and their songs were often heard by rich and poor alike. The song contains typical Celtic themes: the wife from across the sea and the problems of cultural integration. The use of magic spells to forestall a royal birth has its counterpart in the Greek myth of Herakles, where a similarly jealous but divine wife sends the goddess of childbirth

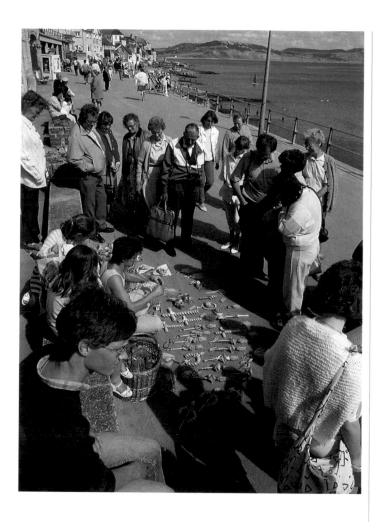

King Willy he's sailed over
  the raging foam,
He's wooed a wife and he's
  brought her home.
He wooed her for her long
  golden hair,
His mother wrought her a
  mighty care:
And a weary spell she's laid
  on her,
She be with child full long
  and many's the year,
But her child she would never
  bear.
And in her bower she lies in
  pain,
King Willy at her bedhead he
  do stand
As down his cheeks the
  salten tears do run.

King Willy back to his
  mother he did run,
And he's gone there as a
  begging son.
He says: 'My truelove has this
  fine noble steed
'The like of which you ne'er
  did see:
'At every part of this horse's
  mane
'There's hanging fifty silver

BELOW **Martin
Carthy.** *The English
solo singer and guitarist
also performs with the
Watersons, Dave
Swarbrick, and John
Kirkpatrick, all of them
pioneers in the revival of
English folk song and
dance. His songs range
from the collected folk
material of the Celtic
fairy and British
historical past to the
contemporary lyrics of
Leon Rosselson, on
subjects such as
Britain's war with
Argentina over the
Falkland Islands.*

ABOVE **Corn-dolly
seller, Lyme Regis,
Dorset, England.** *The
Celts relied heavily on
agriculture, and many
sacrificial rituals were
linked to the continuing
fertility of the land.
Until recently, the last
sheaves of corn during
harvest used to be
plaited into figures or
talismans which
contained the spirits of
the corn. The associated
religious ritual died long
ago, but the dollies
survive as a country
craft; they are still
widely believed to bring
'good luck'. This
craftsman is making a
selection of pagan and
Christian motifs
including horseshoes and
crosses.*

to delay the birth of her husband's mortal
son: the delay allows a rival prince to be
born first and thus to claim the throne
over Herakles. What we would now
term 'witchcraft' was originally Celtic
pagan religious lore and ritual, suppres-
sed by Christianity. The tying of complex magical knots has its counterpart in
the interwoven forms of Celtic art. The
repetitions originate in the oral tradition
but also increase the ritual atmosphere of
the piece.

The song was recorded by a pioneer
in the English folk-song revival, Martin
Carthy, who sings it to the tune of a
traditional Breton drinking-song, Son ar
Chistr (Song of Cider), which has itself
been recorded by Alan Stivell. The tune
was apparently composed in 1930 by a
Breton piper who is now a Paris tramp.
Such borrowings of tunes and changes of
fortune must also have been present in
the life and work of the ancient Celtic
bards.

bells and ten,
'There's hanging fifty bells
    and ten.
'This goodly gift shall be your
    own,
'If back to my own truelove
    you'll turn again
'That she might bear her baby
    son.'

'O but child, she will never
    lighter be,
'Nor from sickness will she
    e'er be free;
'But she will die and she will
    turn to clay,
'And you will wed with
    another maid.'
And sighing, says this weary
    man,
As back to his own truelove
    he's gone again:
'I wish my life was at an end.'

King Willy back to his
    mother he did run
And he's gone there as a
    begging son.
He says: 'My truelove has this
    fine golden girdle,
'Set with jewels all about the
    middle.
'At every part of this girdle's
    hem
'There's hanging fifty bells
    and ten
'There's hanging fifty silver
    bells and ten,
'This goodly gift shall be your
    own,
'If back to my own truelove
    you'll turn again
'That she might bear her baby
    son.'

'Oh but child, she will never
    lighter be,
'Nor from sickness will she
    e'er be free;
'But she will die and she will
    turn to clay,
'And you will wed with
    another maid.'
And sighing, says this weary
    man,

As back to his own truelove
   he's gone again:
'I wish my life was at an end.'

Well up and spoke his noble
   queen;
And she has told King Willy
   of a plan
How she might bear her baby
   son.
She says: 'You must go, get
   you down to the market
   place,
'And you must buy you a loaf
   of wax;
'And you must shape it as a
   babe that is to nurse
'And you must make two eyes
   of glass.
'Ask your mother to the
   christening day,
'And you must stand there
   close as you can be,
'That you might hear what
   she do say."

King Willy, he's gone down
   to the market place,
and he has bought him a loaf
   of wax;
And he has shaped it as a
   babe that is to nurse,
And he has made two eyes of
   glass.
He asked his mother to the
   christening day,
And he has stood there close
   as he could be,
That he might hear what she
   did say.
And how she stormed and
   how she swore:
She's spied the babe where no
   babe could be before,
She's spied the babe where
   none could be before.

She says: 'Who was it undid
   the nine witch-knots,
'Braided in amongst this
   lady's locks?
'And who was it who took
   out the combs of care,
'Braided in amongst this
   lady's hair?

LEFT **Green Man: capital of door column of the Church of St Mary and St David, Kilpeck, near Hereford, England** (*twelfth century* AD). *The pagan fertility god was used to 'scare away the evil eye' in many medieval Christian churches. His staring eyes and the tendrils emerging from his mouth demonstrate the continuing stylistic traditions of Celtic art.*

'And who was it slew the
   master kid,
'That ran and slept all
   beneath this lady's bed,
'That ran and slept all
   beneath her bed?
'And who was it unlaced her
   left shoe?
'And who was it that let her
   lighter be,
'That she might bear her
   baby boy?'

And it was Willy who undid
   the nine witch-knots,
Braided in amongst this lady's
   locks.
And it was Willy who took
   out the combs of care,
Braided in amongst this lady's
   hair.
And it was Willy the master
   kid did slay,
And it was Willy who
   unlaced her left-foot shoe,
And he has let her lighter be.
And she has poured out a
   baby son,
And prayed to the blessings
   that be them upon,
And prayed to the blessings
   them upon.

FURTHER READING

MYTHS, LEGENDS AND FOLKTALES

Most of the following translations and versions are readily available in paperback:

Barber, R (ed), *The Arthurian Legends* (Woodbridge and Wolfeboro, 1979)

Beroul, *The Romance of Tristan* (trans. A S Fedrick; Harmondsworth, 1970)

A Celtic Miscellany (trans. K H Jackson; Harmondsworth, 1971)

Early Irish Myths and Sagas (trans. J Gantz; Harmondsworth, 1981)

Gottfried von Strassburg, *Tristan* (trans. A T Hatto; Harmondsworth, 1960)

The Mabinogion (trans. G Jones and T Jones; illustrated by Alan Lee; Hendrik-Ido-Ambacht, 1982)

The Mabinogion (trans. J Gantz; Harmondsworth, 1976)

Malory, *Le Morte d'Arthur* (Harmondsworth, 1969)

Rolleston, T W, *Myths and Legends of the Celtic Race* (London, 1985)

Scott, M, *Irish Folk and Fairy Tales Omnibus* (Harmondsworth, 1989)

The Tain (trans. T Kinsella; Dublin 1969 and London 1970)

Williamson, R, *The Craneskin Bag: Celtic Stories and Poems* (Edinburgh, 1989)

Wilson, B K, *Scottish Folk-Tales and Legends* (Oxford, 1954)

SUITABLE FOR YOUNGER READERS

Jacobs, J (ed), *Celtic Fairy Tales* (London, 1970)

Cooper, S, *The Dark is Rising Sequence* (London 1984)

Dickinson, P, *Merlin Dreams* (illustrated by Alan Lee; London, 1988)

Garner, A, *Elidor* (London, 1965); *The Weirdstone of Brisingamen* (London, 1960); *The Moon of Gomrath* (London, 1963); *The Owl Service* (London, 1967); *Red Shift* (London, 1973)

INTERPRETATION

The following modern studies of Celtic Mythology are also of interest:

Matthews, C, *Mabon and the Mysteries of Britain: An Exploration of the Mabinogion* (London, 1987)

Matthews, J & C, *The Aquarian Guide to British and Irish Mythology* (Wellingborough, 1988)

Rutherford, W, *Celtic Mythology* (Wellingborough, 1987)

Senior, M, *Myths of Britain* (London, 1979)

VARIANT SPELLINGS AND PRONUNCIATION GUIDE

Spellings of Celtic names are inconsistent from source to source. Anglicizations are generally attempts to reproduce the sound rather than the spelling of the words. Here is a selected list of characters and places with some of their variant spellings. Pronunciations are given only for major figures.

PRONUNCIATION KEY:

['] = before stressed syllable; [ch] = ch in Scottish 'loch'; [ou] = Welsh aw as ou in 'out'; [th] = Welsh dd as th in 'there'; [tl] = Welsh ll as tl in 'little'; [oo] = Welsh w as oo in 'cook'; Welsh u and y = i as in 'pill'; Stresses generally come on the penultimate syllable.

MYTHOLOGICAL GROUPS

(A) Arthurian; (I) Irish; (S) Scottish; (W) Welsh

Ailill ['ailitl] (I)
Albain/Albion/Britain
Allen (S) / Ainle (I)
Aod/Aed [id] (I)
Arden (S) / Ardan (I)
Bedwyr ['bedwir] (W) / Bedivere (A)
Bendigeidfran [bendi'gaydfran] / Bran the Blessed (W)
Branwen ['branoowen] (W)
Bricriu ['brikru] (I)
Brigit/Brigit/Bride (I) (S)
Caswallawn [kas'watloun] (W) / Cassivellaunos
Cathbad ['kafuv] (I)
Cei/Cai/Kay/Keu [kai] (A)
Conchobar mac Nessa ['konchovor] (I) / Connachar [conn'acher] (S)
Connla/Conle ['konlle] (I)
CuChulainn/Cú Chulaind [ku'chulinn] (I)
Culhwch ['kilhooch] (W)
Custennin [küs'tenhin] (W)
Dearg ['dayarg] (I)
Deirdriu ['derrdru] / Deirdre ['derrdri] (I)
Efnissien [ev'nissien] (W)
Erin/Ireland
Etain/Édaín ['edain] (I)
Ferchar ['ferchar] (S) / Fergus (I)
Fingula/Fionnuala
Gwalchmai [goo'alchmai] (W) / Gawain (A)
Gwrhyr ['goohrir] (W)
Harddlech/Harlech ['harthlech] (W)
Isolt/Iseult/Yseult/Isolde (A)
Llŷr [tleer] (W)
Manannan ['mannernan] (I)
Manawydan [man'ouithan] (W)
Matholwch [math'olooch] (W)
Medb/Medhbh/Maeve [methv] (I)
Naoisi/Naois ['noisi] (I)
Oifa/Aoife ['ifer] (I)
Ove/Aobh ['iver] (I)
Pryderi [pri'deri] (W)
Pwyll ['pooitl] (W)
Rhiannon [hri'annon] (W)
Sidhe [shee] (I)
Sualtam ['suerllterm] (I)
Twrch Trwyth [toorch'trooeeth] (W)
Uisnech/Usnach ['usnerch] (I)
Yspaddaden [usba'thaden] (W)

Index

Acknowledgements

The author would like to extend special thanks to Gwen for her hospitality, Tony for his archeology, Christina for her images, Joan for her Iseult, Planxty for their music, and Alan Lee for his paintings.

Picture Credits

The author and publishers would also like to thank the following for the use of picture material in this book:

Bath Museum: pages 10 (photo. Fotek), 11, *l*, 11 *r* (photo. Fotek). © **David Bellingham:** pages 16, 18, 28, 44 *b*, 46, 47, 57, 69, 77, 81 *b*, 101 *r*, 109, 112, 113, 117, 122 *t*, 124. **Birmingham Museum and Art Gallery:** pages 86, 90. **The Bodleian Library, Oxford:** page 84. **Musée Calvet, Avignon:** page 68. **City Art Centre, Edinburgh:** page 106. **Claddagh Records Ltd/photo. Janet Williamson:** page 49 *l*. **Commissioners of Public Works, Ireland:** page 42. **C M Dixon, Canterbury:** pages 7 *r*, 9 *l* (British Museum, London), 9 *r*, 17 (The Museum of Antiquities, Newcastle-upon-Tyne University), 19 *l* (Naturhist. Museum, Vienna), 20 (National Museum, Budapest), 21 (National Museum, Copenhagen), 23 *l* (National Museum, Copenhagen), 24 *t b* (National Museum, Copenhagen), 25, 26 *tl* (British Museum, London), 26 *bl r*, 27 (British Museum, London), 32 *l* (Cluny, Paris), 32 *r*, 33, 34, 35–6 (British Museum, London), 39, 41, 43 (Württemberg Landesmuseum, Stuttgart), 44 *t* (British Museum, London), 49 *r* (Victoria and Albert Museum, London), 52 (Prahistorische Staatsammlung, Munich), 53 *t* (The Museum of Antiquities, Newcastle-upon-Tyne University), 53 *b* (British Museum, London), 54 (British Museum, London), 55 (Netherhall Collection) 56, 59 *t* (Bucharest Museum, Romania), 59 *b* (Museum of Antiquities, Newcastle-upon-Tyne University), 60 (National Museum, Copenhagen), 61 (British Museum, London), 63, 65 (British Museum, London), 66 (Viking Ships Museum, Bygdøy, Oslo), 67 (National Museum, Copenhagen), 71 (National Museum of Antiquities, Bucharest), 78 *l* (National Museum, Copenhagen), 78 *r* (British Museum, London), 79 (National Museum, Copenhagen), 80, 82 (National Museum of Wales), 83 (National Museum of Ireland, Dublin), 92, 94 (National Museum, Budapest), 95 (Museum of National Antiquities, Stockholm), 96 *t* (Corbridge Museum, Northumberland), 96 *c*, 96 *b* (Musée Borely, Marseilles), 100 *l*, 103 (National Museum of Antiquities, Stockholm), 105 (British Museum, London), 108 (British Museum, London), 119 (National Museum of Antiquities, Edinburgh), 123. **Dundee Art Galleries and Museums:** pages 29, 45. **General Post Office, Dublin:** page 23 *r*. **Glasgow Art Gallery and Museum:** page 37. © **C Grande:** pages 102, 115, 120. **Hayling Island Excavation Project/photo. G Soffe:** page 72 *t*. **Humberside County Council Archeology Unit:** page 19 *r*. © **Tony King:** pages 7 *l*, 8 *r*, 72 *b*, 73 *t b*, 74–5, 110. **Lambeth Palace Library/MS 6, f.43 v, © 1981 LPL/photo. Mike Gunn:** page 107. © **Alan Lee:** pages 64, 81 *t*, 93. **Peter Nahum Ltd:** page 87. **The National Gallery of Ireland:** pages 12, 118. **The National Museum of Ireland:** page 111. **National Galleries of Scotland, Edinburgh:** pages 15, 38, 97. © **Quintet Publishing Ltd/photo. Trevor Wood:** pages 31, 51. **Skyscan Balloon Photography Copyright:** pages 6, 22, 62, 100 *r*. **Topic Records/photo. Dave Peabody:** page 122 *b*. **Trinity College Library, Dublin:** page 48. © **Sheree Wilson:** page 8 *l*.

Front jacket: Gundestrup Cauldron, Denmark (National Museum, Copenhagen).
Back jacket: Scorhill Bronze-Age stone circle, Dartmoor, England (David Bellingham).